BONHOEFFER:
Worldly Preaching

BONHOEFFER:
Worldly Preaching

CLYDE E. FANT

THOMAS NELSON INC., PUBLISHERS

Nashville, Tennessee / New York, New York

Library of Congress Cataloging in Publication Data

Fant, Clyde E
    Bonhoeffer: worldly preaching.

    Includes bibliographical references.
    1. Preaching—History. 2. Bonhoeffer, Dietrich, 1906–1945.
BV4207.F36   230′.092′4   74–26806
ISBN 0–8407–5087–0
ISBN 0–8407–5586–4 pbk.

To the Church
at Ruston

Dietrich Bonhoeffer

1906   Born in Breslau, Germany, to Karl and Paula von Hause Bonhoeffer on February 4

1923   Studied at University of Tübingen

1924   Toured Rome and North Africa; began study at University of Berlin

1927   Presented the *Communion of Saints* for the licentiate degree in theology

1928   Pastored German colony in Barcelona, Spain

1930   Submitted *Act and Being* as entrance dissertation of a beginning professor, University of Berlin; arrived in New York for study at the Union Theological Seminary as a Sloane Fellow

1931   Met Karl Barth; appointed youth secretary for the World Alliance for Promoting International Friendship through the Churches; ordained; began work with confirmation class in North Berlin

1933   Helped develop the Confessing Church in opposition to Hitler's church policies; became pastor of German-speaking congregation in London

1935   Called to head a seminary for the Confessing Church

1937   Gestapo closed the seminary; *The Cost of Discipleship* published

1941   Became an important part of the resistance movement in Germany

1943   Arrested on April 5 and placed in military prison

1945   Hanged on April 9 at Flossenbürg

Clyde E. Fant and William M. Pinson, *20 Centuries of Great Preaching*, vol. 12 (Waco: Word Books, 1971), p. 93.

Contents

Preface

During my research for an article on the preaching of Dietrich Bonhoeffer in *20 Centuries of Great Preaching,* I became intrigued with the lectures on homiletics which he delivered to the tiny Confessing Church seminary at Finkenwalde. These lectures were as yet untranslated into English and at that time I had never seen any reference to them. (Since then I have seen less than a half-dozen references in either English or German works, none extensive.) As a matter of fact, their existence seemed generally not to be known, and so I decided to translate them to make their significant ideas available to English-speaking readers.

But as such things have a way of doing, one thing led to another, and this book is the result. As the work progressed, I became increasingly convinced that Bonhoeffer's interest in the traditional concerns of practical theology—the place of preaching, pastoral care, and worship in the church—was by no means limited to these lectures or to passing references in his larger themes. It soon became obvious that these concerns were central. Only his involvement with Christology could challenge them for preeminence in his writings, and that question was so closely bound with the other that the two are virtually inseparable.

This conclusion will not be particularly surprising to Bonhoeffer specialists, though their works have largely dealt with other aspects of his thought. But among many non-specialists and laymen there continues to be a persistent feeling that Bonhoeffer was anything but a "churchman"—if, in fact, he did not outright demand a "churchless" Christianity—and that whatever Christians might accomplish in the world in the future would take place through individual *caritas* alone and apart from ecclesiology. It should come as no surprise then, in any game of theological password, that "Bonhoeffer" as a clue does not call forth "preaching" as a response.

It would be utterly untrue to Bonhoeffer's sharp criticisms of the church and its speaking to attempt to gloss over these elements in his theology. But it is equally false to extract these remarks from the total context of his theology, even that expressed from his prison cell, and ignore the driving concerns which motivated them. This work would be completely misunderstood if it were seen as ignoring Bonhoeffer's strongest critiques of the church and its proclamation, or as treating them with less than the utmost seriousness they deserve. That stance would not only be untrue to Bonhoeffer's contribution, it would be absolutely perilous for both preaching and the church.

Likewise, however, we must treat with equal seriousness Bonhoeffer's obvious and continuous commitment to the proclamation of the Word as the task of a purified church—indeed, as the means for its renewal. This is the only way to prevent the world from making a religion of itself and thereby losing its chance for true worldliness.

In the last of his theological letters from prison which we possess, Bonhoeffer expressed his weariness and even his own shock with the negative aspect of his latest works and his eagerness to get on to more positive reconstructions. It is our loss that he never lived to do so. But it is my feeling that the church has also reached that same point of weariness. It is high time to see the point behind all of the sharp points which Bonhoeffer thrust at the church—his passionate desire for the renewal of a church which he loved to the last. He never gave up his daily devotion to the Scripture and prayer as the instruments of "God's guiding hand" (letter of Aug. 31, 1944—the last which we have) and his steadfast belief in the coming day when men would be "called upon to utter the word of God that the world will be changed and renewed by it" (May, 1944).

I am grateful to many people for their encouragement and assistance in this effort. Particularly must I express my appreciation to Eberhard Bethge for his careful consideration of my theme and his encouragement. It was a privilege to examine Bonhoeffer's original manuscripts and to discuss both sides of that correspondence with their recipient. I will never forget the many courtesies extended to me during my visit to Rengsdorf. Likewise, Prof. Dr. Dietrich Rössler of Eberhard-Karls University, Tübingen, willingly gave many hours in his home in discussion of the subjects explored in this work. Dr. Scott Bartchey of the New Testament department at Tübingen also provided a number of helpful suggestions.

This book would have been completely impossible without the dedicated work of Mrs. Kara Hammer, who was so much more than a typist in the trans-Atlantic production of the manuscript. My research assistant, Maynard Campbell, also rendered invaluable service in locating and sending various Bonhoeffer materials otherwise unavailable. Günter Schnöring took many hours away from preparation for his terminal exams in theology at Tübingen to read and discuss my translation of Bonhoeffer's lectures, and I am grateful for his suggestions. I must also add a word of personal thanks to our beloved German friends, the Jung family, for their constant support and love, and for the wonderful relaxation which their gracious home provided. Again, I am greatly appreciative for the encouragement and support of Vester Hughes and The Foundation for Christian Communication.

Finally, to my family who endured with patience the ridiculous interruption of writing a book during a year in Europe—thanks.

PART ONE

*How Can the Church Speak
to the World?*

The Message through Preaching?

The prominence of preaching in the life and thought of Dietrich Bonhoeffer can scarcely be overestimated. In the fourth volume of Bonhoeffer's collected works in German (Gesammelten Schriften, Band IV), the volume which contains Bonhoeffer's sermonic works, Eberhard Bethge writes:

> The conclusion of the *Collected Works* may be the high point of these works. To be sure, the preaching of Bonhoeffer was not the sensation of the past decade—his deeds and his insights created the excitement. But Bonhoeffer acted and analyzed out of a responsibility for preaching . . . the Bonhoeffer who taught, the Bonhoeffer who was obedient to the Word, the Bonhoeffer who was involved, was governed by preaching and its majesty.
> That does not seem to be very modern; but that the words of God should come from the mouths of men is His miracle.[1]

In fact, Bethge insists that for Bonhoeffer, "Discipleship, suffering, silence, worldliness— all that does not take the place of the sermon, but serves for its enthronement" (p. 9). These more familiar concepts have largely occupied the attention of the previous writings on Bonhoeffer, so that the place of proclamation in Bonhoeffer's thought is not prominent in current writings on his religious (or nonreligious) concepts.

It is true that Bonhoeffer struggled with the helplessness in which the word had found itself in his time, and he preferred

1. Dietrich Bonhoeffer, *Gesammelten Schriften,* ed. Eberhard Bethge, 5 vols. (Munich: Chr. Kaiser Verlag, 1961), IV:11–12; hereafter, **GS**. Most *ibid.* references are indicated by parenthetical page numbers instead of footnotes.

to fall silent rather than saying too much or becoming too cautious. Yet he "never doubted the coming of the new enthronement of the Word, under which the world would be 'renewed and transformed' " (p. 8). His concern for the sermon "was not a matter of fearfulness" but of confidence in the ultimate value of the sermon. "The 'secular interpretation of biblical concepts' does not mean the discontinuation of preaching, but the first step toward its renewal for the world" (p. 12). Again, "While today the content of the sermon has become vague and its form has been adjusted according to the influences of liturgy and mass psychology, Bonhoeffer stands unshaken upon the irreplaceability of the preaching of the Christ" (p. 7). The word of the sermon possesses a "majesty" which can be replaced by nothing else because it both "has and is the presence of Christ."

Nor was this concept simply an "empty dogma" or "sterile teaching," against which Bonhoeffer so often spoke. The separation between thought and life for Bonhoeffer was unthinkable. His practice bore equal witness to his confidence in the sermon: "Bonhoeffer loved to preach. When a relative discovered that she might have only months to live, he wrote: "What would I do if I learned that in four to six months my life would reach the end? I believe I would still try to teach theology as I once did and *to preach often*" (p. 7). (This statement is all the more significant because it was written during the silence enforced on him by the government in the summer of 1940.)

Bonhoeffer had indeed correctly analyzed his own deepest concerns: "At the end, the word of the Gospels stands above everything, biographically and factually. On the day before his death Bonhoeffer preached one more time, without ornamentation, liturgy, or religious trappings for a few Protestants, Catholics, agnostics, and atheists" (p. 11).

Bethge insists that those who would use Bonhoeffer's last words from prison as the crowning blow against the sermon misunderstand him: " 'To preach often' not only appeared meaningful for him, it was his most certain reality in the face of death. The word of the sermon has, and is, the presence of Christ" (p. 7).

Bethge attributes the misunderstanding of Bonhoeffer at this point to the fragmentation of his thinking, an "atomization" of the total picture of Bonhoeffer. Bonhoeffer's work does not limit itself to the realm of any single group of specialists. Therefore to the theological specialist Bonhoeffer is too much the preacher and to the preacher Bonhoeffer is too much the theologian. For the theologian, the preacher is always technically too imprecise and humanly too specific; while to the ecclesiastical practitioner, the theologian is too troublesome because he watches everything too closely, and often critically. The writings of Bonhoeffer will never completely satisfy either of these groups. Nor, with all of the emotional element removed, will his life. The tensions remain, the puzzling and often tantalizing expressions, the ambiguities, and even, at points, the contradictions.

These very elements, however, have been Bonhoeffer's provocation and stimulation to contemporary theology. In Germany, this stimulation has led largely to investigations concerning interpretation and hermeneutic, while in the English speaking countries attention has been largely directed toward ecclesiological and ethical questions. Any attempt to so divide his thought, however, will only result in frustration: "It is the unity (not the unification) of the three elements—theology, ecclesiology, and ethics—that so attracts one to Bonhoeffer. He can hardly fail to disquiet anyone who yields to the temptation to resolve the tension of these elements in favor of any one of them." [2]

How then shall Bonhoeffer be understood? Obviously approaches may be, and have been, made from any one of several directions. Word, church, world—these, in many variations of expression, are Bonhoeffer's chief concerns. No one may dominate over another without damage being done to the wholeness of Bonhoeffer's thought. Is there a connecting link, a unifying thread which binds the three of these concepts into a meaning-

2. Bonhoeffer, *Letters and Papers from Prison*, rev. ed., ed. by Bethge (New York: Macmillan Co., 1967), p. xiii; hereafter, LPP.

ful whole? It may not be flatly asserted that Bonhoeffer's concern for proclamation is the only such possible unifying concept, but preaching is so fundamental to an understanding of Bonhoeffer that Bethge could assert, "Preaching is the focal point in the picture of Bonhoeffer in its three stages. In the first stage he was concerned about the concreteness of the Word, in the second, about its costliness, and in the third about its worldliness." [3] By these three stages Bethge intends to suggest, roughly, the early academic period (terminating in Berlin in 1932); the subsequent period of ministry prior to his imprisonment (terminating in his return to Germany from the United States in July, 1939); and the final stage, the time of his imprisonment and *Letters and Papers from Prison* (terminating in his execution by the Nazis). [4]

Each of his dominant concepts—Word, church, and world—must be examined to see if indeed proclamation is a unifying concern in each; but first, a brief examination of Bonhoeffer's personal involvement with preaching may serve to further illustrate the unity which proclamation provides in his life and thought. Only after letting his life serve as commentary upon his words are we ready to hear and correctly interpret his most striking words: "With Bonhoeffer, actions and life comment on his sayings, and the words on his actions, in an extraordinary degree." [5]

Bonhoeffer's Life: A Commentary on Words

Godsey describes Bonhoeffer as "a man for whom preaching was an integral part of life." [6] He did not approach his pro-

---

3. GS, IV:11.

4. For a thorough study of these three periods in Bonhoeffer's life, see "The Challenge of Dietrich Bonhoeffer's Life and Theology" by Bethge in The Chicago Theological Seminary *Register*, LI:2 (Feb., 1961).

5. Ibid., p. 26.

6. John D. Godsey, *The Theology of Dietrich Bonhoeffer* (Philadelphia: Westminster Press, 1960), p. 92.

fessional life, however, from the same direction as many other theologians—for example, Karl Barth—from the pulpit to the lecture hall, but from the lecture hall to the pulpit. The contrast between Barth and Bonhoeffer at this point is interesting:

> Karl Barth was a Swiss pastor at first, involved in the social struggle of his congregation, moving later into the academic world. Bonhoeffer, imbedded in highly bourgeois academic surroundings, started as the obvious future professor, living in the distinguished company of scholars; then he strove after the practical involvements of the ministry, to the slight disappointment of his father and the bitter regret of his colleagues. . . . Barth, though highly systematic, started with sermon and biblical exegesis and went, though still highly exegetical, into dogmatics. Bonhoeffer started completely as a dogmatic theologian and moved into a period of nearly exclusively exegetical interest. (This interest, it should be mentioned, was not the interest of the historian who wants to clarify objectively the old sources as such but the personal commitment of the exegetical preacher who, in accepting the claim of the authority of the Scripture, witnesses the biblical truth to contemporary minds.) [7]

Barth's movement from the pulpit to the professorship had its own remarkable significance and has been often commented upon; but the implications of the relationship between the professorship and the pulpit in the life of Bonhoeffer, in some ways even more remarkable than in the life of Barth, should also not be overlooked.

Once the transition was made, the effect on Bonhoeffer was profound. Speaking of his later ministry in Berlin, Bethge said, "Preaching was the great event in his life; the hard theologizing and all the critical love of his church were all for its sake, for in it the message of Christ, the bringer of peace, was proclaimed.

7. Bethge, "The Challenge of Dietrich Bonhoeffer's Life and Theology," p. 6.

To Bonhoeffer nothing in his calling competed in importance with preaching." [8]

The way to the pulpit for Bonhoeffer was not accompanied by much encouragement. His brilliant record as a student opened for him the possibility of an academic career as well as a life of activity in the church. His family took it for granted that he would choose the academic career, particularly since there was little doubt that he could be certain of swift and sure advancement. Unlike other students, who struggled in vain to leave the pastorate for teaching, Bonhoeffer faced another problem: "His problem was not how to enter the academic world, but how to escape from it. The pulpit appealed to him more than the professor's chair" (p. 68). In fact, from the beginning even his decision to enter the Christian ministry was not met with great enthusiasm. His father, at first disappointed by this decision, later commended him for his choice:

> When I heard that you intended to enter the pastorate as a boy, I thought that this was not the way that you should go, confining yourself to a corner of life. I thought at the time that such a removed and unreal existence as a pastor as I knew it from my uncle was too small; it was a pity that you would do that. Now, seeing the Church in a crisis that I never thought would be possible, I see that what you have chosen was very right.[9]

Subsequent to his graduation, Bonhoeffer's initial work found him as an assistant pastor to a German community in Barcelona, Spain, in the year 1928. To some extent his pastoral experience in Barcelona was limited, but not with regard to practice in the writing and delivering of sermons, "which he regarded as the mainspring of his office." [10] The preaching of these sermons was

8. Bethge, *Dietrich Bonhoeffer,* ed. Edwin Robertson, trans. Eric Mosbacher, Peter and Betty Ross, Frank Clarke, and William Glen-Doepel (New York: Harper & Row, 1970), pp. 174–75.

9. William Kuhns, *In Pursuit of Dietrich Bonhoeffer* (London: Burns & Oates, 1967), p. 8.

10. Bethge, *Dietrich Bonhoeffer,* p. 78.

"accompanied by the pleasure of youthful discovery" (p. 175).

Nevertheless, Bonhoeffer worked hard on his preaching. In a letter to his parents dated November 27, 1928, he wrote, "Writing sermons still takes up a great deal of my time. I work on them a whole week, devoting some time to them every day." He was pleased when the minister was away and gave him the opportunity to fill the pulpit: "On the first Sunday in Advent I shall be able to preach again because Olbricht will not be returning until the following week and I am very pleased about that." Writing on the seventh of August, 1928, to Helmut Rössler, a contemporary and former fellow student, he said: "Now during the summer, when I am alone for three months, I have been preaching once a fortnight. And I find the same thing as you. I don't know what to do with the precious half hours which we have; I preach more different things than I would ever have thought possible." [11]

In the same letter he listed the texts from which he was preaching: Romans 11:6; 1 Corinthians 15:14–17; Matthew 28:20; 1 Thessalonians 5:17; Luke 12:49; Matthew 7:1; Psalm 62:2; 1 Corinthians 12:26ff; Matthew 5:8. Bonhoeffer delivered his sermons on these texts enthusiastically, if not always with exegetical accuracy. The congregation that heard these messages probably missed a great deal of their significance, largely due to the complexity of language with which they were clothed. Nevertheless they were not without effect: "Even though the sermons that Bonhoeffer preached so passionately to the Barcelona congregation to a great extent passed far over their heads, he nevertheless spoke to them as one who, during the week, visited them and filled them with a warmth and pastoral concern to which they were unaccustomed." [12]

As he would later recommend to others in his Finkenwalde lectures on homiletics, Bonhoeffer did not limit himself to the recommended pericopes, but always spoke from brief texts.

11. Bonhoeffer, *No Rusty Swords,* ed. Edwin H. Robertson, trans. Edwin H. Robertson and John Bowden (New York: Harper & Row, 1965), p. 38.

12. Bethge, *Dietrich Bonhoeffer,* p. 79.

(Later he would tend to preach from longer passages.) There was a great thematic unity to these early sermons in Barcelona. Fourteen of his sermons and three lectures which he delivered in the Christmas holidays have been preserved, and they reveal many of the themes which would later be dominant in his thinking: the insistence upon man's dependence upon God's grace; the reminder that the Christian must not forsake the world ("If you want to find God, be faithful to the world"); the concern for the Christian's relationship with his fellowman; the victory of Christ crucified; and already, attention to the word which would later create great controversy and excitement, the word "religion." [13]

In the light of his later works, his most interesting reference to the word "religion" occurs in a sermon preached on Romans 6, March 11, 1928, "It is not religion that sets us right with God, for God alone can do this; it is His action upon which we must depend." Equally significant is a remark made in an unpublished lecture—"Jesus Christ and the Nature of Christianity"—:

> The Christian religion as a religion is not of God. It is on the contrary another example of a mortal road to God like the Buddhist or any other, although of course different in form. Christ is not the bringer of a new religion, but the bringer of God, therefore as an impossible road from man to God the Christian religion stands as other religions; the Christian can do himself no good with his Christianity, for it remains human, all too human, but he lives by the grace of God, which comes to man, and comes to every man, who opens his heart to it and learns to understand it in the Cross of Christ; so the gift of Christ is not the Christian religion, but the mercy and love of God which culminate in the cross. (p. 73).

Some emphases in these youthful sermons are familiar to his later works, such as the themes just enumerated, but other elements are more distinctively a part of this period of his life. In

13. Mary Bosanquet, *The Life and Death of Dietrich Bonhoeffer* (London: Hodder and Stoughton, 1968), p. 72.

these sermons he made more frequent personal references than he ever again made; his language is dramatic, almost flowery; and he made much more extensive use of illustration, analogy, and comparison than in his later sermons. He did not depend upon news items or politics for illustrative material, but he drew from more classical sources: "He picked what suited him from the world of his education—Heraclitus, the giant Antaeus from the world of antiquity, or Goethe's and Nietzche's anthropological analyses from the nineteenth century. In his first and last sermons at Barcelona—and several in between—he quoted St. Augustine on the heart that is unquiet 'until it resteth in thee.' Similarly Barth's Tower of Babel often recurs as a key example to show the dangerousness of 'religion.' " [14]

There may also be somewhat more of an interest in the evaluations of others on his preaching during this Barcelona period than will later be true; though certainly no unhealthy interest manifested itself, only the natural curiosity of the young minister who is not yet quite certain of his own reactions to self-satisfaction and his feelings of success:

> I am thankful that I am able to have some measure of success in it. It is a mixture of subjective pleasure, shall we say self-satisfaction, and objective gratitude—but that is the judgment of all religion, this mixture of the subjective and the objective, which we may possibly enoble somewhat, but which we can never completely eliminate, and the theologian suffers doubly from this—but on the other hand, should one not rejoice in a full church or over the fact that people are coming again who had not come to church for years; and on the other hand, who dares to analyze this pleasure and feel quite certain that it is free from the seeds of darkness? [15]

There is much that is familiar in these early sermons also, including the characteristic tension between the subjective and objective as in the quotation immediately preceding. Other ele-

14. Bethge, *Dietrich Bonhoeffer*, pp. 79–80.
15. GS, I:51–52.

ments are equally familiar: the grappling with difficult texts; the struggle to express vividly and specifically upon the hearers that which struggled for expression within his own mind; his sensitivity with the hurts of the modern world; his appreciation of nature and of life itself; his personal confession of the importance of Bible reading, devotional meditation, and silence in his own experience.[16] Furthermore, Bethge asserts that these early sermons reveal "the whole gamut of his theological work and outlook": [17] (1) he continually reiterates the antithesis between faith and religion; (2) he emphasizes the presence of Christ and the church; (3) he points to the importance of the concrete and the earthly.

Beyond these common links with his future works, Bonhoeffer also seems to have made a fundamental discovery concerning preaching during his days in Barcelona:

> For a long time I thought that there was a central point in preaching, which, once one touched on it, could move anyone or confront them with a decision. I don't believe that anymore. First, preaching can never apprehend the central point but can only be apprehended by it, by Christ. So Christ becomes flesh as much in the words of the pietists as in those of the churchmen or the Christian socialists, and these empirical restrictions mean not relative, but in fact absolute difficulties for preaching; men are not the same even at the deepest level, but they are individuals, totally different and only "united" by the Word in the church. I have noticed that the most effective sermons were those in which I spoke enticingly of the Gospel, like someone telling children a story of a strange country. The difficulty in principle remains: one should give milk, but one doesn't know what that means and wonders whether one isn't giving sugared water by mistake.[18]

16. Sermon on Psalm 42:1, preached July 15, 1928.
17. Bethge, *Dietrich Bonhoeffer*, p. 80.
18. *No Rusty Swords*, p. 38.

This insight had profound significance for the next two interludes in his life, his visit to America and his experiences in
Berlin; where on the one hand he will say in America that
he is hearing sermons which are "sugared water," and in Berlin, where he will seek to declare the gospel to individuals
under the most difficult of circumstances without himself falling victim to watered-down preaching.

Before beginning his academic career at the University of
Berlin, Bonhoeffer spent a year in America as Sloane Fellow
at Union Theological Seminary where he took courses under
Niebuhr, Lord, Lyman, and Baillie.[19] There is actually not
much to be said about Bonhoeffer's contact with preaching
during this first American visit, and what is to be said is
almost entirely negative. In New York he was shocked to discover that preaching had been "degraded to marginal ecclesiastical observations about events of the day," "the quoting
of edifying instances . . . willing descriptions of one's own
religious experiences, to which of course no binding character is attributed in practice." [20]

Bonhoeffer's suspicion of the continual citing of one's own
religious experience—a theme which would recur frequently
in his writings—is evident in this statement concerning the
preaching of the American students at Union Seminary: "Because the American student sees the question of truth essentially in the light of practical community, his preaching becomes an edifying narration of examples, a ready recital of
his own religious experiences, which are not of course assigned
any positively binding character. . . . If the first sermons of
the German student serve for him to hand on his dogmatics as
quickly as possible, they serve for the American student to
display before the congregation the whole of his religious
experience." [21]

19. For a complete listing of the specific courses which Bonhoeffer
took while at Union Seminary, see Hans J. Hillerbrand, "Dietrich Bonhoeffer and America," *Religion and Life* XXX:4 (Autumn, 1961): 568.

20. GS, I:77, 86, quoted in Bethge, *Dietrich Bonhoeffer*, p. 175.

21. *No Rusty Swords*, p. 88.

He was also not impressed by Fosdick, even though he termed him "one of the most influential American preachers," except that Bonhoeffer recognized him as one professor who did at least seek to deal with the question of the church's message, but one who nevertheless answered this question "in an extreme humanistic sense."

Bonhoeffer's impressions of preaching in American Christianity reflect the same criticisms made of the preaching at Union Seminary. All of the sermons which he heard, whether preached in a Baptist church, a synagogue, or a community church, had the same characteristics: they sought to speak to the contemporary situation, but identified contemporary preaching with socio-political comments; an endless variety of secular themes might be displayed, but one would have difficulty in hearing sermons on the cross, sin, forgiveness, or even the gospel itself; and traditional Christian dogma was denounced freely from the pulpit. Furthermore, the church itself was no longer the place where the congregation hears the word of God; it was a social club. Christianity in America could be described as nothing more than an ethical idealism, and the true purpose of the church had been forgotten; "teas, lectures, concerts, charity events, athletics, dances, and bowling for all ages are substituted for the proper work of the church." [22]

With this unsavory impression of American church life in general and its preaching in particular, Bonhoeffer returned to Berlin for a brief interlude as theological professor as well as preacher.

In the fall of 1931 Bonhoeffer began teaching at the University of Berlin. He did not completely abandon his pastoral work, however; he also served as the student chaplain at the Technical Institution of Charlottenburg, a suburb of Berlin. In November he began teaching a confirmation class of forty boys from a poverty-stricken area of the city. Sometime during this same year Bonhoeffer's spiritual life underwent a momentous change. The change is all the more remarkable in the

22. Hillerbrand, "Dietrich Bonhoeffer and America," p. 570.

light of his own often-stated reservations concerning the subject of "conversion":

> Then something happened, something that has changed
> and transformed my life to the present day. For the first
> time I discovered the Bible. . . . I had often preached, I
> had seen a great deal of the Church, and talked and
> preached about it—but I had not yet become a Christian.
> . . . Also I had never prayed, or prayed only very little.
> For all my abandonment, I was quite pleased with myself.
> Then the Bible, and in particular the Sermon on the
> Mount, freed me from that. Since then everything has
> changed. I have felt this plainly, and so have other people
> about me. It was a great liberation. It became clear to
> me that the life of a servant of Jesus Christ must belong
> to the Church, and step by step it became plainer to me
> how far that must go.[23]

Whatever the nature of this personal experience, it certainly had no ill effects upon his preaching. At this time he was preaching at regular intervals in the university church, a preaching which he took intensely seriously. His sermons began to develop an urgency which had not been characteristic of them before, an urgency that insisted upon a single-minded devotion to Christ.

The critical events of those days caused Bonhoeffer to insist that this devotion must not be compromised through fear. In a sermon preached on Sunday evening, January 15, 1933, in the Church of the Trinity he spoke against such fear. His text was Matthew 8:23–27, the experience of Jesus stilling the storm and quieting the fears of the disciples in the boat. In a sermon packed with imagery, and even emotion, he said:

> But now in the midst of this world of fear a place has
> been established which has as its own particular task—

23. Bethge, *Dietrich Bonhoeffer*, pp. 154–55.

the task which the world cannot understand—to call out
to men one thing, ever the same and ever new: Fear is
overcome; do not be afraid; in the world you have fear,
but be of good cheer, I have overcome the world! Oh
ye of little faith, why are you so afraid? Christ is in the
ship! And this place which is so spoken of is the pulpit
in the church. The living Jesus himself wants to tell the
world from the pulpit that for those in whom he enters,
fear disappears.[24]

This statement leaves no doubt of the role of the pulpit
in relation to the Word, the church, and the world, nor of the
importance of preaching and the sermon to Bonhoeffer during
this period of his life.

Bonhoeffer's dependence upon the Scripture in his preaching became ever clearer, and any text he selected for these
sermons became "a sort of sermon on the situation in itself.
. . . [He] drew just one message from it and impressed this
on his hearers as the theme. Thus, on two consecutive Sundays
. . . he preached two entirely different sermons on the same
brief text from Colossians."[25] The contemporaneity of these
sermons, however, is equally unmistakable, and his applica-
tions pointed and sharp. "Every sermon must be an event,"
as he said to Fritz Hildebrandt. In a sermon preached May
29, 1932, on Luke 16:19–31 (Lazarus and the rich man),
he emphasized the importance of concreteness in proclamation: "We can neither understand nor preach the gospel
tangibly enough. A truly evangelical sermon must be like
offering a child a beautiful red apple or holding out a glass of
water to a thirsty man and asking: Wouldn't you like it?"[26]

He worked hard on these sermons and began his preparation for them well in advance. Then when he had fixed upon
the text and the theme, he wrote out his sermons word for
word and subsequently made few corrections. Many of these

24. GS, IV:105.
25. Bethge, *Dietrich Bonhoeffer*, p. 175.
26. GS, IV:51.

sermons during the Berlin period represent the high point of Bonhoeffer's sermonic work.[27]

In 1933 Bonhoeffer went to London as pastor of the German Evangelical Congregation of Sydenham, London. Although this effort represents a relatively brief interlude in his life, the year and a half he spent in London ministering to German Christians was the only time in his life when he was fully occupied with the parish ministry. No doubt the most significant thing about his London sojourn was not his preaching during this period (although Bethge describes it as ardently "eschatalogical"). His contacts with Bishop Bell and his support for the Church of the Resistance which was developing in Germany were of greater significance. Nevertheless, this period contributed one key experience to Bonhoeffer's understanding of preaching. He learned for the first time the pressures of the pastoral responsibility upon the preaching minister. In May, 1934, he wrote home: "It is really incomprehensible that so much should happen in so small a congregation." Nor did he find it easy to preach twice on a Sunday.[28] Later, in his homiletical lectures to the students at Finkenwalde, he made reference to these pressures and the necessity for the minister to continue to devote sufficient time to his sermon preparation in spite of them.

During his years in London, Bonhoeffer dreamed of a trip to India. That dream was never realized, and instead he accepted the call to train the theological students for the Confessing Church in Germany. On April 26, 1935, Bonhoeffer began this work. The group met at first at Zingst, on the Baltic, but the accomodations were not good, and so in June of that year the work was moved to Finkenwalde, near Stettin. The desire for community life in this effort has been well

27. For a more complete description of a number of these sermons see Bethge, *Dietrich Bonhoeffer*, pp. 174–78, and Bosanquet, *The Life and Death of Dietrich Bonhoeffer*, pp. 106–8.

28. *I Knew Dietrich Bonhoeffer*, ed. Wolf-Dieter Zimmermann and Ronald Gregor Smith, trans. Kathe Gregor Smith (New York: Harper & Row, 1966), p. 95.

documented, but the place of preaching and the training of the preacher were equally prominent in it. In a paper written by Bonhoeffer on the sixth of September, 1935, and addressed to the Council of the Church of the Old Prussian Union, he stated the purposes of a community house within the general structure of the Confessing Church. Numerous statements refer to the prominence of preaching in this endeavor:

1. The pastor, and particularly the young pastor, suffers from being by himself. The burden of preaching is particularly heavy today for the solitary pastor who is not a prophet, but just a servant of the church. He needs brotherly help and fellowship not only to show him what he is to preach, but also to show him how to preach it. . . . Preaching which has its roots in practical work, as well as in the life and experience of the community, will be more relevant, and less likely to run the risk of either being intimidated or bogged down.

2. The nature of the Christian life is again being questioned by the younger generation of theologians. . . . The damage done to the credibility of our preaching by our life and by our uncertainty as to what Christian life is compels us to think again and to embark upon new practical ventures.

3. There is a need for a group of completely free, trained pastors to preach the Word of God for decision and for discerning the spirits, in the present church struggle and in others to come, and to be immediately ready to serve as preachers at the outbreak of any new emergency. . . .

The brethren of the community live together with a strict liturgical ordering of their day. . . . A common theological and ecclesiastical consideration of preaching and the Word of God in the Bible will keep them down-to-earth and practical.[29]

29. Bonhoeffer, *The Way to Freedom*, ed. Edwin Robertson, trans. Edwin H. Robertson and John Bowden (New York: Harper & Row, 1966), pp. 29–31.

Bonhoeffer's personal interest with these questions is easily documented: "Bonhoeffer would sometimes entrust the discussion of sermons to his assistant, but the actual teaching of homiletics he always reserved for himself." Again, "Nothing, he insisted, is more concrete than the real voice of Christ speaking in the sermon." [30]

At first it seemed strange to the students that their homiletical efforts, however hesitant and faltering, should be so seriously treated as the true voice of Christ. But day by day their confidence grew, not in themselves, but in the Word of God, and few of them returned to the preaching task without an increased respect and happiness in the task of preaching. In a great measure this was due to Bonhoeffer's personal insistence upon the place of the pulpit: "Bonhoeffer did not advocate exchanging the pulpit for the academic rostrum for he believed that the former must regain an independence which cannot be exchanged. It is true that he appreciated the academic rostrum insofar as it acted as corrective to the sermon, but it never made the sermon superfluous" (p. 363).

Perhaps from this Finkenwalde period one further footnote should be added, that is, with reference to Bonhoeffer's regard for the importance of *listening* to sermons. He worked hard at listening to sermons; Bonhoeffer "loved to hear other preachers." It was not easy for someone as sensitive and scholarly as Bonhoeffer to educate himself to listen to simple messages, but "even in the poorest attempts from the pulpit, he succeeded in looking for and finding the divine message." [31] Bethge suggests that Bonhoeffer's students seem to have been influenced more by his concept of the proper hearing of the sermon than by his methodological suggestions for preaching.

One reason for this influence was likely Bonhoeffer's insistence that any sermon preached before a congregation at a worship service at Finkenwalde must be listened to in all humility and not be analyzed. "The only sermons he allowed

---

30. Bethge, *Dietrich Bonhoeffer,* p. 361.
31. GS, IV:7.

to be discussed were those that were read aloud, never those that had been delivered before a congregation; about the latter he might, on rare occasions, say a word in private. . . . Needless to say he gave due attention to problems of method and form, but nothing exerted so chastening an effect as Bonhoeffer's method of listening to sermons. He himself demonstrated daily what he required in the way of expression, taste, and imaginativeness. Thus homiletics began with the most difficult lesson of all—one's own listening to sermons." [32]

Bonhoeffer's own sermons during this time were startlingly direct and demanding. Many of these were mimeographed and circulated among the former students of the community, and they have been termed "exceptional expositions of scripture from the heart and mind of a man for whom preaching was an integral part of life." [33] This circular letter, or *Rundbrief,* was sent out each month from Finkenwalde until the outbreak of the war. It reported on the whereabouts and the various activities of the former students and gave news and events of the developments at Finkenwalde, listed the texts chosen for the morning meditations, and provided drafts of sermons (often Bonhoeffer's own), and hints for their preparation. "These latter were especially appreciated by those of us who had entered the parish ministry: the brotherly assistance they gave helped us to avoid the danger of preaching a purely parochial gospel." [34]

In September of 1937 Finkenwalde was closed by order of Himmler. In November of that year twenty-seven of the men from Finkenwalde were arrested. Bonhoeffer for some reason, was not arrested. During the following year of increasing political involvement and contact with leaders of the political resistance, Bonhoeffer continued to emphasize in his personal

32. Bethge, *Dietrich Bonhoeffer,* p. 361.
33. Godsey, *The Theology of Dietrich Bonhoeffer,* p. 92.
34. Paul F. W. Busing, "Reminiscences of Finkenwalde," *Christian Century,* LXXVIII (Sept. 20, 1961): 1110.

letters and in his lectures the importance of the minister's fidelity to true proclamation in the midst of the turmoil within the church (see, for example, the address delivered to a conference of "illegal" younger theologians in Pomerania in October, 1938).[35]

His brief visit to America during approximately this same period (1939) did not do anything to improve his evaluation of American preaching. Bonhoeffer criticized most of the sermons he heard during his four-week visit to the United States. His diary for Sunday, June 18, 1939, records:

> Service in Riverside Church. Quite unbearable. Text: a saying from James (!) about "accepting a horizon"....
>
> The whole thing was respectable, self-indulgent, self-satisfied religious celebration. This sort of idolatrous religion stirs up the flesh which is accustomed to being kept in check by the Word of God. Such sermons make for libertinism, egotism, indifference. Do people not know that one can get on as well, even better, without "religion" —if only there were not God himself and his Word? Perhaps the Anglo-Saxons are really more religious than we are, but they are certainly not more Christian, at least, if they still have sermons like that. I have no doubt at all that one day the storm will blow with full force on this religious hand-out, if God himself is still anywhere on the scene. Humanly speaking the thing is by no means unattractive, but I prefer the rustic preaching of Br. Schultz. The tasks for a real theologian over here are immeasurable. But only an American himself can sift all this rubbish, and up till now there do not seem to be any about (pp. 230–31).

On the other hand, a sermon he heard on that same evening at Broadway Presbyterian Church from Dr. McComb on "Our Likeness with Christ" received his commendation, and was even termed "astonishing": "A completely biblical sermon.

35. *The Way to Freedom,* pp. 173–93.

. . . This will one day be a centre of resistance when Riverside Church has long since become a temple of Baal. I was very glad about this sermon. . . . This sermon opened up to me an America of which I was quite ignorant before" (p. 231). Nevertheless, this was the only positive report Bonhoeffer could make on the American sermons he heard. On June 24, 1939, he wrote in his diary: "Tomorrow is Sunday. I wonder if I shall hear a *sermon?*" The answer came in the next entry, Sunday, June 25: "Service in the Lutheran church. Church on Central Park, Dr. Scherer. Sermon on Luke 15, on the overcoming of fear. Very forced application of the text. Otherwise lively and original, but too much analysis and too little Gospel. It came home when he said of the life of the Christian that it is like the daily joy of the person who is on the way home. Again no real exposition of the text" (p. 237). The last sermon which he heard in America was on July 2, 1939. He wrote, "Church, Park Avenue. Rev. Gorkmann (Radio preacher) on 'Today is ours,' no text, no echo of the Christian proclamation. Rather a disappointment" (p. 240).

Bonhoeffer did note, however, that the optimistic, evolutionary view of man in American theology had disappeared, but he wondered if it had not been replaced by an overly pessimistic view. In either case he criticized the lack of a biblical stance. He quoted President Coffin of Union as saying that Niebuhr "preaches for half an hour on the 'failure of man' and the last two minutes on the 'grace of God.'" Bonhoeffer noted, "If that is generally true, they are now where we were fifteen years ago." As for Coffin himself, Bonhoeffer described him as a "straightforward, practical man" and made this interesting observation about him, "He sees the necessity of preaching the Gospel" (p. 227).

In spite of their negative nature, it is apparent from Bonhoeffer's comments on America and American preaching that his priorities concerning the sermon as the medium through which God's message should be proclaimed were still very much intact.

Bonhoeffer returned to Germany in late July, 1939. Between this date and his arrest by the Gestapo in April of 1943, his activities in teaching and preaching were increasingly restricted. At first he served as something of a visiting preacher in the northern German provinces, but by the summer of 1940 the government prohibited him from any further preaching. The following year he was forbidden to print or publish any of his writings.[36]

But even during this time of increased political activity and increasing disappointment with the church's failure to speak out, he never lost his desire to preach. He surprised himself by a lack of interest, sometimes for days at a time, in his lifelong practice of Bible reading and prayer. Yet eventually his zeal for such things, and for preaching, always returned: "Again and again I am driven to think about my activities which are now concerned so much with the secular field. I am surprised that I live and can live without the Bible for days. . . . If I open the Bible again after such a period, it is new and rewarding as ever and *I eagerly want to preach once again.*" [author's own italics] [37]

36. This period in Bonhoeffer's life is succinctly described by Bethge in "The Challenge of Dietrich Bonhoeffer's Life and Theology," Chicago Theological Seminary *Register*, Feb., 1961, pp. 26–28.

37. Ibid., p. 29. This particular letter, written by Bonhoeffer in June, 1942, as he was returning from Stockholm, has been incorrectly identified as one of Bonhoeffer's letters from prison [in the article by Otto Dudzus, one of Bonhoeffer's former students, "Discipleship and Worldliness in the Thinking of Dietrich Bonhoeffer," *Religion and Life*, XXXV (Spring, 1966): 239.] There is a very similar reference to Bonhoeffer's occasional disinterest in Bible reading in LPP, p. 128, but it is obviously not the same: "Once again I am having weeks when I don't read the Bible much; I never know quite what to do about it. I have no feeling of obligation about it, and I know, too, that after some time I shall plunge into it again voraciously. May one accept this as an entirely 'natural' mental process? I'm almost inclined to think so. . . . But it would be wrong to get anxious about it; we can depend upon it that after the compass has wobbled a bit, it will point in the right direction again."

Following his imprisonment by the Gestapo in 1943, Bonhoeffer's personal involvement with proclamation obviously drew to a close. But there were a few exceptions: his "Wedding Sermon from a Prison Cell"; his "Thoughts on the Baptism of D. W. R." (Dietrich Wilhelm Rudiger Bethge, the son of Eberhard Bethge, who was named for him); and the last, tragic sermon preached on Sunday, April 8, 1945—the day before his death. There were a few other tangible evidences of his continued proclamation. A fellow prisoner recalled how Bonhoeffer had continued to minister to others: "Many little notes he slipped into my hands on which he had written biblical words of comfort and hope." [38]

His final sermon deserves fuller comment. Payne Best, a British secret service agent, described this last sermon:

> Pastor Bonhoeffer held a little service and spoke to us
> in a manner which reached the hearts of all, finding just
> the right words to express the spirit of our imprisonment
> and the thoughts and resolutions which it had brought.
> He had hardly finished his last prayer when the door
> opened and two evil-looking men in civilian clothes came
> in and said: "Prisoner Bonhoeffer, get ready to come with
> us." Those words "come with us"—for all prisoners they
> had come to mean one thing only—the scaffold. We
> bade him good-bye—he drew me aside—"This is the
> end," he said. "For me the beginning of life." [39]

In addition to these few contacts with preaching, his letters from prison contain many intriguing references to preaching—both positive and negative—which help us to understand the place of proclamation in Bonhoeffer's often-cited utterances during his last days. But at this point we must now turn from

38. Fabian von Schlabrendorff, "In Prison with Dietrich Bonhoeffer," *I Knew Dietrich Bonhoeffer*, p. 228.
39. S. Payne Best, *The Venlo Incident* (London: Hutchinson, 1950), p. 180.

an examination of Bonhoeffer's life as commentary upon his words to a study of his words as a commentary upon his life.[40]

2

Words and the Word

Not only would it be difficult to attempt to describe Bonhoeffer's concept of the Word apart from preaching, it would be virtually impossible. For Bonhoeffer, Christ not only *says* the Word, he is the Word. He does not stand behind the sermon, he is present in the spoken word of preaching:

> Christ is not only present *in* the word of the church but also *as* the word of the church, i.e. as the spoken word of preaching. *"In* the word" might say too little, if it made it possible to separate Christ from his Word. Christ's presence is his existence as preaching. The whole Christ is present in preaching, Christ humiliated and Christ exalted. His presence is not that power of the community or its objective spirit from which the preaching is made, but his existence as preaching. Were that not so, preaching could not have the prominent place accorded to it by the.

40. For related articles concerning Bonhoeffer's preaching see: concerning his method, Fant, Clyde E., Jr., and William M. Pinson, Jr., "Dietrich Bonhoeffer," *Twenty Centuries of Great Preaching,* Vol. XII Marshall to King (Waco, Texas: Word Books, 1971), pp. 105ff., and GS, IV:7–12; concerning his hermeneutics, see the essay by R. Grunow in *Die mündige Welt,* Vol. I (Munich: Chr. Kaiser Verlag, 1955), pp. 62ff., *I Knew Dietrich Bonhoeffer,* pp. 128, 133, 140; for evaluations of his preaching which also comment upon his use of the scripture, see *The Place of Dietrich Bonhoeffer,* pp. 127–32, and Dietrich Ritschl, *A Theology of Proclamation* (Richmond, Va.: John Knox Press, 1960), pp. 169ff.

Reformation. This place belongs to even the simplest
preaching. Preaching is the riches and the poverty of the
church. It is the form of the presence of Christ to which
we are found and to which we have to keep.[1]

What relation is sustained between God's Word and man's
words in preaching? It is not one of exclusiveness: "The human word of preaching is not a phantom body for the Word
of God. But the Word of God has really entered into the
humiliation of the word of man" (p. 53). God has voluntarily
entered into man's word of preaching as the Word of God.
With reference to the sermon, Bonhoeffer paraphrased slightly
an expression of Luther and said, "You shall point to this
word of man and say, 'That is the Word of God.'" Pointing
to the sermon is pointing to Christ among his people. "Christ
is present in the church as the spoken Word, not as music
and not as art." Bonhoeffer insists that the subjectivity—not
the identification—with reference to the Word must be equally
asserted along with its objectivity. "Two things must be said
here with equal emphasis: 'I could not preach if I did not
know that I were speaking the *Word of God';* and 'I could not
preach did I not know that *I* were not speaking the Word of
God.'"

The Progress of an Idea

In his earliest works, this theme is consistently emphasized.
Like Luther, Bonhoeffer saw the Word of God in the Scrip-
ture and in preaching; and like Luther, he located the pres-
ence of Christ even more specifically in preaching than in the
Bible: "The Word is concretely present in the church as the
Word of Scripture and of preaching—essentially as the lat-
ter." [2] Again, "The Word is the Word the church preaches.
Not the Bible, then? Yes, the Bible, too, but only in the church.

1. Bonhoeffer, *Christology,* intro. Edwin H. Robertson, trans. John
Bowden (London: Collins, 1966), p. 52.
2. Bonhoeffer, *The Communion of Saints,* trans. R. Gregor Smith
(New York: Harper & Row, 1963), p. 161.

So it is the church that first makes the Bible into the 'Word'? Certainly, insofar, that is, as the church was first created and is maintained by the Word." Commenting on these remarks, Godsey says, "That is, the Spirit has not bound himself substantially with the word of the Bible, where the definite promise of fruitfulness is attached to the word preaching in the *sanctorum communio* (Isaiah 55:11)." [3]

In another early work, *Act and Being*, Bonhoeffer described three sociologically different functions of the church: believing knowledge, preaching knowledge, and theological knowledge. As Christ is preached in the congregation, he gives himself to the church member. *Believing knowledge* is therefore knowing that one has been forgiven by the person of Christ through the preached word. *Preaching knowledge,* on the other hand, is what the preacher knows about what he preaches. But this knowledge is not a mere collection of facts, but an experiential knowledge of the crucified Christ. It is true that the preacher must reflect upon propositions and historical words, but when the preacher declares these words and propositions which have been entrusted to him, the living Christ testifies to himself through them. *Theological knowledge* is the memory of the church. But as such, dogma is not the goal of the sermon but the presupposition upon which preaching is founded. These three forms of knowledge working together serve to protect the revelation of God from the presumption of man. In the same work, Bonhoeffer reminded the church that "the Word of this community is preaching and sacrament, its conduct is believing and loving." [4]

Similarly, in 1932 at a conference in Switzerland Bonhoeffer said, "Christ must become present to us in preaching and in the sacraments just as in being the Crucified One he has made peace with God and with men." [4] This note is sounded uniformly throughout his early works.

3. Godsey, *The Theology of Dietrich Bonhoeffer,* p. 48.

4. Bonhoeffer, *Act and Being,* intro. Ernest Wolfe, trans. Bernard Noble (New York: Harper & Row, 1961), p. 125.

5. *No Rusty Swords,* p. 187.

In two of his best known works from his "middle period," Bonhoeffer continued to insist upon preaching as the locus of the Word. In *The Cost of Discipleship* (1937) he asserted that the preaching of the church and the administration of the sacraments is the place where Jesus Christ is to be found:

> If we would hear his call to follow, we must listen where he is to be found, that is, in the church through the ministry of Word and sacrament. The preaching of the church and the administration of the sacraments is the place where Jesus Christ is present. If you would hear the call of Jesus you need no personal revelation: all you have to do is hear the sermon and receive the sacrament, that is, to hear the gospel of Christ crucified and risen. Here he is, the same Christ whom the disciples encountered, the same Christ whole and entire. Yes, here he is already, the glorified, victorious and living Lord. Only he himself can call us to follow him.[6]

In *Life Together* (1939) his principal emphasis was not upon the *official* act of the church in proclamation, that is the office of preaching, but upon what Bonhoeffer termed "the ministry of proclaiming." However, he did briefly discuss the true authority of the preacher and of the bishop, an authority not to be located in the "cult of personality," but in the "simple servant of the Word of Jesus Christ" who has the confidence of the church because it recognizes that it is being guided by "the Word of the Good Shepherd."[7]

Beyond this "official" function of proclamation in the church, however, Bonhoeffer sought to extend the responsibility for proclaiming to the community at large through a "ministry of proclaiming." He defined the ministry of proclaiming as "the free communication of the Word from person to person, not

6. *The Cost of Discipleship*, pp. 201ff.
7. Bonhoeffer, *Life Together*, trans. and intro. John W. Doberstein (New York: Harper & Bros., 1954), pp. 108–9.

by the ordained ministry which is bound to a particular office, time, and place. We are thinking of that unique situation in which one person bears witness in human words to another person." This ministry is fraught with many dangers, but Bonhoeffer cannot imagine that true brotherhood is possible without speech one to another: "Where Christians live together the time must inevitably come when in some crisis one person will have to declare God's Word and will to another. It is inconceivable that the things that are of utmost importance to each individual should not be spoken by one to another" (p. 105).

The basis for such speech is our understanding of the brother's need as a sinner and the dignity that he has to share in God's grace and glory. We may speak to one another on the basis of the help which we both need; we must be both gentle and severe with one another; we must not be afraid of one another, since we have only God to fear. We must also learn the discipline of listening to God's word from others. We must not become touchy and sensitive, or else we will soon become flatterers and will come to despise and slander our brothers. Reproof is therefore as unavoidable as encouragement, and we must learn to give and to take both. Such proclaiming is the solemn responsibility in the fellowship: "He has put His Word in our mouth. He wants it to be spoken through us. If we hinder His Word, the blood of the sinning brother will be upon us. If we carry out His Word, God will save our brother through us" (p. 108).

Bonhoeffer's identification of preaching with the presence of the Word is well established in these earlier works, but what of his later, more critical writings? This question must largely be answered in the context of Bonhoeffer's challenging questions to the church and of the world: Is the church the place for preaching, the place for the Word of God; and does the "world come of age" have any need for preaching? The next two sections of this work will examine these questions in some detail. But perhaps three quotations from his last works may serve to establish the continuity of his thought with reference to the preeminence of preaching as a medium for the Word.

The first comes from Bonhoeffer's *Ethics,* an uncompleted book from Bonhoeffer's last years, published posthumously by Eberhard Bethge after having been assembled from fragments. This was to be the major work of Bonhoeffer. It was his driving concern during his last days, and he worked on it as often as he could under the trying circumstances in which he found himself. With reference to proclamation, he writes:

> The word which came from heaven in Jesus Christ
> desires to return again in the form of human speech. . . .
> God himself desires to be present in this word. God
> Himself desires to speak His word in the Church.
>
> What the Church proclaims is the word of the
> revelation of God in Jesus Christ. This word does not
> proceed from any man's own heart or understanding or
> character; it comes down to man from heaven, from the
> will and the mercy of God; it is a word commanded and
> instituted by Jesus Christ. . . . In the place of God
> and of Jesus Christ there stands before the congregation
> the bearer of the office of preaching with his
> proclamation.[8]

The second comes from Bonhoeffer's famous *Letters and Papers from Prison.* In May, 1944, in his "Thoughts on the Baptism of D. W. R." in the same paragraph where his often-quoted expression "our earlier words are therefore bound to lose their force and cease . . .", these lines bring the article to a conclusion: "It is not for us to prophesy the day (though the day will come) when men will once more be called on to utter the Word of God that the world will be changed and renewed by it. It will be a new language, perhaps quite non-religious, but liberating and redeeming—as was Jesus'

8. Bonhoeffer, *Ethics,* ed. Bethge, trans. Neville Horton Smith (London: SCM Press, 1955), p. 259. The major portion of his *Ethics* was written by Bonhoeffer between 1940 and 1943.

language; it will shock people and yet overcome them by its power; it will be the language of a new righteousness and truth, proclaiming God's peace with men and the coming of his kingdom." [9] Bonhoeffer could foresee a time of difficulty for proclamation, a time of silence and struggle; but in the end, it will once again be the proclaimed word which will change and renew the world, and it was toward this end that Christians should pray.

The third quotation from Bonhoeffer's late works comes from "The First Table of the Ten Commandments," an uncompleted work written during June and July of 1944. It is the next to the last work from Bonhoeffer which exists (the last work is the poem, "The Death of Moses," written in September of 1944). Its impact is all the more striking because it was being written at precisely the same time (during the months of June and July, 1944) when Bonhoeffer was writing his letters that later attracted so much attention, the letters in which his most famous expressions, "the world come of age," "religionless Christianity," and "the nonreligious interpretation of biblical concepts," first appeared.[10] The following excerpt is from "The Third Commandment," "Remember the sabbath to keep it holy" (in German, "You shall hallow the holiday"):

> The consecration of the holiday occurs through the proclamation of the Word of God in worship and through the willing and respectful hearing of this Word. The desecration of the holiday begins with the deterioration of Christian proclamation. The guilt for this desecration is therefore first of all the guilt of the church and particularly of its ministers. Thus the renewal of the consecration of this holiday must begin with the renewal of preaching.[11]

9. LPP, p. 161.

10. These questions were first taken up in the letter of April 30, 1944, and then came to their high point in the letters of May 25, 1944, June 8, 1944, June 30, 1944, July 8, 1944, July 18, 1944, and in his "outline for a book" written in a letter of August 3, 1944.

11. GS, IV:611.

Eight months, then, before his death, Bonhoeffer continued in his unwavering conviction that the preaching and the hearing of the Word causes the Sabbath to be consecrated and that only the renewal of preaching can begin the needed renewal of the consecration of the Sabbath.

The church in general and preaching in particular cannot evade the difficult questions posed by Bonhoeffer in his last writings. But neither should anyone ignore the fact that to the very end Bonhoeffer identified the coming of the Word of God, with all of its renewing power for the church and for the world, with preaching.

Before going on to examine the implications of these problems for preaching with reference to the church and the world, a brief examination of some of Bonhoeffer's statements regarding authority, revelation, and the Bible may be of further value in clarifying the relationship between the divine Word and human words in Bonhoeffer's thinking.[12]

Authority, Revelation, and the Bible

If proclamation occupies such a key role in the Christian faith, where does the authority for such proclamation lie? [13] First of all, it does not reside in the preacher himself: "In sociological terms, in the sermon God's claim of authority is made plain to his congregation. . . . But the preacher himself does not have this authority—this belongs to the Word which he speaks. Jesus in his preaching combined personal and objective authority, but not so the preacher." [14]

12. Notice that these questions are also dealt with extensively in Bonhoeffer's Finkenwalde Lectures on Homiletics, contained in Part Two of this work.

13. Does proclamation mean more to Bonhoeffer than the Sunday sermon? Gerhardt Ebeling writes, " 'Proclamation' obviously must not only be understood as the Sunday sermon, but certainly includes it more especially." *Word and Faith*, trans. James W. Leitch (Philadelphia: Fortress Press, 1960), p. 120.

14. *The Communion of Saints*, p. 165.

Throughout his works Bonhoeffer made it clear that authority should not be equated with the individual minister, nor with the personal experiences of Christians, still less with the "cult of personality": "Jesus made authority in the fellowship dependent upon brotherly service. Genuine spiritual authority is to be found only where the ministry of hearing, helping, bearing, and proclaiming is carried out. Every cult of personality that emphasizes the distinguished qualities, virtues, and talents of another person, even though these be of an altogether spiritual nature, is worldly and has no place in the Christian community; indeed, it poisons the Christian community." [15] The church must be especially careful not to place its confidence in either human wisdom or human conceit, but rather in the "simple servant of the Word of Jesus Christ," because it knows then that it will be led by "the Word of the Good Shepherd."

Genuine authority, therefore, does not reside in brilliance or attractiveness; indeed, in the man himself there may be nothing to admire. True authority resides in the one who properly exercises his ministry. The necessary trust which the community must have in its preacher, a matter closely related to that of authority, is only determined by the faithfulness with which he serves Jesus Christ and not by the extraordinary talents which he may possess: "Pastoral authority can be obtained only by the servant of Jesus who seeks no power of his own, who himself is a brother among brothers submitted to the authority of the Word."

Nevertheless the congregation must respect the office of preaching and must recognize that it has been established by Jesus Christ himself. "It is established *in* the congregation and not *by* the congregation, and at the same time it is *with* the congregation." [16] The faithful congregation will recognize the

15. *Life Together,* p. 108.
16. *Ethics,* p. 259. This statement represents a distinct and important shift in Bonhoeffer's thought. Earlier (*The Communion of Saints*) he had said that the communion of saints founded the office of preaching.

distinctive place given to the office of preaching within it and will do everything possible to serve it:

> The congregation which is being awakened by the
> proclamation of the Word of God will demonstrate the
> genuineness of its faith by honouring the office of
> preaching in its unique glory and by serving it with
> all its powers; it will not rely on its own faith or on
> the universal priesthood of all believers in order to
> deprecate the office of preaching, to place obstacles
> in its way, or even to try to make it subordinate to
> itself. The superior status of the office of preaching is
> preserved from abuse, and against danger from without,
> precisely by genuine subordination of the congregation,
> that is to say, by faith, prayer and service, but not by
> suppression or disruption of the divine order or by
> perverse desire for superiority on the part of the
> congregation.[17]

It may sound surprising to hear Bonhoeffer refer to "superiority" and "inferiority" with reference to the respective roles of preaching and listening within the congregation. No deprecation is meant. It is simply a matter of obedience on the part of the preacher to the task to which God has called him (proclaiming) and on the part of the congregation to its task (hearing):

> Above there is the office of proclamation, and below
> there is the listening congregation. In the place of God
> and of Jesus Christ there stands before the congregation
> the bearer of the office of preaching with his proclamation.
> The preacher is not the spokesman of the congregation,
> but if the expression may be allowed, he is the spokesman

For further comment on this question, see Jürgen Moltmann and Jürgen Weissbach, *Two Studies in the Theology of Bonhoeffer,* trans. Reginald Fuller and Ilse Fuller (New York: Charles Scribner's Sons, 1967), p. 57.
   17. *Ethics,* p. 260.

of God before the congregation. . . . When this office is
exercised in the congregation to its full extent, life is
infused into all the other offices of the congregation,
which can after all only be subservient to the office of
the divine word; for wherever the word of God rules
alone, there will be found faith and service (pp. 259–60).

If the responsibility of the congregation is to respect the
office of preaching, then the responsibility of the preacher is to
proclaim his message without uncertainty. Neither of these
responsibilities proceeds from the personal esteem of self-
assurance of the preacher himself; both are duties laid upon
the church by Christ. This confidence in proclamation requires
a certain kind of knowledge on the part of the preacher: "The
preacher, as one who addresses the communion, must 'know'
what he preaches: Jesus Christ the Crucified (1 Corinthians
2:2). . . . There may be no uncertainty here, no not-knowing:
all must be made plain from the Word of God who has bound
himself in revelation, for in the preaching which produces
faith Christ causes himself to be declared the 'subject' of the
spoken words." [18] The preacher must remember that he is
only able to preach in the strength of Christ, in the strength
of the knowledge that he has been forgiven within the community wherein revelation occurs. This thought serves to re-
mind the preacher of his dependence upon Christ in proclamation and to encourage his true humility with reference to the
Word.

Bonhoeffer therefore suggests that revelation only takes
place through the present proclamation of the life and death
of Jesus Christ, and furthermore that this revelation only takes
place within community. Revelation must not be located in a
unique occurrence in the past, in some objective entity which
has no connection with our present existence. Nor can it be
conceived as a nonobjective act which occasionally touches
the existence of individuals: "Revelation, then, happens within

18. *Act and Being,* p. 142.

the communion; it demands primarily a Christian sociology of its own. The distinction between thinking of revelation individualistically and thinking of it in relation to community is fundamental. . . . Today, therefore, it can only be a question of the Christ preached in the Church, his death and resurrection" (pp. 122–23).

When Bonhoeffer speaks of community, he means by that the church: "The community in question is concretely visible, is the Christian Church which hears and believes the preaching of the Word" (p. 125). The event of Jesus Christ is therefore an event within community and not simply an individual existential encounter. The proclamation of the church is "thus the impingement of the future upon man, rather than a journey into the dead past of the original being of his creaturely-existence. The church starts from what actually happens when Jesus Christ takes form as community." [19]

Nevertheless, this coming of Christ to his community in the form of proclamation is no second incarnation; the Christ which is proclaimed is the real Christ walking in the midst of his people:

> The presence of the already given God-man Jesus is concealed for us, and exists in the *scandalon* form of proclamation—a stumbling block to the Jews (1 Cor. 1:23). The proclaimed Christ is the real Christ. This proclamation is not a second incarnation. The offense caused by Jesus Christ is not his incarnation—that indeed is revelation—but his humiliation. . . . Now that means for us that Christ is present as the Risen and Exalted One only in proclamation, and that means at the same time: only by way of a new humiliation. In proclamation the risen and exalted one is thus present in his humiliation.[20]

19. André Dumas, *Dietrich Bonhoeffer: Theologian of Reality,* trans. Robert McAfee Brown (New York: Macmillan Co., 1968), p. 108.
20. *Christology,* pp. 46–47.

For Bonhoeffer, this is a key concept: The proclaimed Christ is the real Christ. In proclamation, Jesus Christ again takes form as the Incarnate One who endures humiliation. And the more that the church, or the preacher, or the proclaimed word, participates in this humanness, all the more is that evidence of the true humanity of Christ manifesting itself anew in the midst of his people. Preaching, with all of its very human limitations, is therefore indissolubly bound to the presence of Christ among us.

Closely related to this issue is a question with which Bonhoeffer long struggled—the question of concreteness in proclamation.[21] It is essential to understand that for Bonhoeffer there can be no question of "making the message concrete." Jesus, who in his earthly life took the utter risk of human concreteness, takes this risk again within proclamation, within the church as his body. Since Christ is present in the message, that is true concreteness.

Bethge explains that to speak of the "concrete nature" of the sermon is not to describe a recommended ingredient in proclamation, but an essential fact about it. Concretion in proclamation is not dependent upon the minister with his greater or lesser degree of gifts, nor upon his methodology in application. "Concreteness is to be understood not as an addition or second activity but as a genuine attribute of revelation itself." [22] Bethge insists that we completely miss Bonhoeffer's point if we understand it as "the quest for *making* the message concrete." He defines concreteness as being essential to and a genuine attribute of revelation, and includes temporality, historicity, involvement, and the realities of the day.[23]

21. For a further discussion of the question of concretion in proclamation see the "Excursus" by that title in Bonhoeffer's Finkenwalde Lectures on Homiletics in Part Two of this work.

22. Bethge, "The Challenge of Bonhoeffer's Life and Theology," p. 7.

23. For a further discussion of concretion in proclamation, see Ernst Feil, *Die Theologie Dietrich Bonhoeffers* (Verlag Kaiser-Grünewald, 1971), pp. 111ff.

Yet Bonhoeffer never denied the necessity for the preacher's personal involvement in making the message specific and tangible. Those who studied under him report that he taught them "to speak colorfully." [24] Bonhoeffer himself said, "The gospel cannot be preached . . . tangible enough." [25] But relevance must not simply be reduced to a matter of quoting news items or citing events of the day, much less adducing one's own personal experience as evidence of true contemporaneity. Bonhoeffer identified relevance with far deeper concerns, with ultimate matters, with the particular interests of the Word of God itself.

Such relevance proceeds from the Word of God to us; we do not bring it to the Word of God, as though it were hopelessly mired in ancient history without us. He writes: "Where Christ is spoken of in the word of the New Testament, relevance is achieved. *The relevant* is not where the present age announces its claim before Christ, but where the present age stands before the claims of Christ, for the concept of the present age is determined not by a temporal definition but by the Word of Christ as the Word of God. The relevant has no feeling of time, no interpretation of time, no atmosphere of time, but the Holy Ghost, and the Holy Ghost alone. The relevant is and begins where God himself is in his Word." [26]

Therefore Bonhoeffer could say that the most essential element of the Christian message and of the exposition of the scriptural text is not the human act of interpretation, but the act of the Holy Spirit in the Word; indeed, it is God himself. Therefore this does not occur "outside or alongside" the word of Scripture, but exclusively and entirely through it; through "being factual," that is, through the faithful adherence of preaching to the Scripture.

24. *I Knew Dietrich Bonhoeffer,* p. 111.
25. GS, IV:51.
26. "The Interpretation of the New Testament," *No Rusty Swords,* p. 311.

But at this point another question must be raised. How does the Bible relate to the question of revelation and authority in proclamation? Bonhoeffer's absolute respect for the Bible as the Word of God in his own devotional life, his insistence upon the importance of reading it and knowing it (his own detailed knowledge of it at times borders upon the incredible), and his place for it with respect to the proclamation of the gospel is to be observed in virtually every page of his writings. In particular we might mention those passages in *Letters and Papers from Prison* where he repeatedly emphasizes his devotional use of the Scripture and its sustaining power for him in his darkest days. Furthermore, numerous passages in *Life Together* typify his consistent emphasis upon the importance of reading and knowing the Bible. For example:

> Consecutive reading of biblical books forces everyone who wants to hear to put himself, or to allow himself to be found, where God has acted once and for all for the salvation of men. We become a part of what once took place for our salvation. . . . And only insofar as we are *there,* is God with us today also. . . . In this light the whole devotional reading of the Scriptures becomes daily more meaningful and salutary. What we call our life, our troubles, our guilt, is by no means all of reality; there in the Scriptures is our life, our need, our guilt, and our salvation. . . . Only in the Holy Scriptures do we learn to know our own history. . . . We must learn to know the Scriptures again, as the Reformers and our fathers knew them. We must not grudge the time and the work it takes. . . . But one who will not learn to handle the Bible for himself is not an evangelical Christian.[27]

In the same vein, Bonhoeffer delivered a paper in the summer of 1932 entitled "The Church Is Dead" (in answer to that accusation which had been made to him by "a serious Ger-

27. *Life Together,* pp. 53–55.

man") at a conference on the church in Gland, Switzerland. With reference to the Bible, he said:

> Let me express to both groups the great concern which
> has been bearing down on me with growing heaviness
> throughout the whole conference; has it not become
> terrifyingly clear again and again, in everything that
> we have said here to one another, that we are no longer
> obedient to the Bible? We are more fond of our own
> thoughts than of the thoughts of the Bible. We no longer
> read the Bible seriously, we no longer read it against
> ourselves, but for ourselves. If the whole of our conference
> here is to have any great significance, it may be perhaps
> that of showing us that we must read the Bible in quite
> a different way, until we find ourselves again.[28]

Even with reference to the critical problems of the Bible, Bonhoeffer refused to allow the search for a "perfect hermeneutic" to obstruct proclamation.[29] In his *Christology* he wrote: "We must be ready to admit the concealment in history and thus accept the course of historical criticism. But the Risen One encounters us right through the Bible with all its flaws. We must enter the straits of historical criticism. Its importance is not absolute, but at the same time it is not a matter of indifference. In fact it never leads to a weakening of faith but rather to its strengthening, as concealment in historicity is part of Christ's humiliation." [30]

Bonhoeffer therefore recognized the necessity for historical criticism, but he only saw the difficulties which it posed as part of the "humiliation" of Christ, an essential part of his taking flesh and dwelling among us in the present interpretation and proclamation of the ancient word.

In fact, Bonhoeffer termed Bultmann's attempt to reduce Christianity to its essence ("the typical liberal process of re-

28. *No Rusty Swords,* pp. 185–86.
29. See particularly GS, IV:8–10.
30. *Christology,* p. 76.

duction") as a mistake: "You cannot, as Bultmann supposes, separate God and miracle. . . . Bultmann's approach is fundamentally still a liberal one (i.e. abridging the gospel) whereas I am trying to think theologically." [31] He did not recognize the gospel as the essence clothed in mythological garb, but rather the whole matter was the gospel itself: "My view is that the full content, including the 'mythological' concepts, must be kept—the New Testament is not a mythological clothing of a universal truth; this mythology (resurrection etc.) is the thing itself—but the concepts must be interpreted in such a way as not to make religion a precondition of faith (cf. Paul and circumcision)" (p. 172). For Bonhoeffer, the supernatural is simply an indispensable part of the message itself.[32]

Of course the office of proclamation itself is inseparable from the Bible. In fact, Bonhoeffer makes the rather surprising observation that the Bible belongs most properly to the office of preaching:

> The office of proclamation, the testimony to Jesus
> Christ, is inseparably bound up with Holy Scripture.
> At this point we must venture to advance the proposition
> the Scripture is essentially the property of the office of
> preaching and that it is the preaching which properly
> belongs to the congregation. Scripture requires to be
> interpreted and preached. By its nature it is not a book
> of edification for the congregation. What rightly belongs
> to the congregation is the text of the sermon together
> with the interpretation of this text, and on this basis
> there is a "searching of the Scriptures, whether these
> things be so" (Acts 17:11), that is to say, whether they
> are really as the preaching has proclaimed them to be;

31. LPP, p. 143.

32. For a further discussion of this question, see Kenneth Hamilton, *Revolt Against Heaven* (Grand Rapids: William B. Eerdmans, 1965), pp. 172ff. and William O. Fennell, "Dietrich Bonhoeffer: The Man of Faith in a World Come of Age," *Canadian Journal of Theology,* VIII (July, 1962): 178–79.

in certain unusual circumstances, therefore, there arises
the necessity for contradicting the preaching on the basis
of Holy Scripture.[33]

Bonhoeffer additionally goes to great lengths to insist that this
statement by no means implies the prohibition of Bible reading on the part of the congregation, but is only a matter of
the recognition of the place which is essentially appropriate
to the Scripture. As Godsey puts it, "Bonhoeffer merely wants
to emphasize the essential and primary relation of the Scripture to the office of proclamation." [34]

It may be useful for further reference to quote here the
statement from *The Communion of Saints* which has been
previously cited concerning the Word and the Bible:

> So it is the church that first makes the Bible into the
> "Word"? Certainly, insofar, that is, as the church was
> first created and is maintained by the Word. The question
> as to what came first, the Word or the church, is
> meaningless, because the Word as inspired by the Spirit
> exists only when men hear it, so that the church makes
> the Word just as the Word makes the church into the
> church. The Bible is the Word only in the church, that is
> in the *sanctorum communio*. The Word is concretely
> present in the church as the word of Scripture and of
> preaching—essentially as the latter. There is no distinction
> between these in themselves, since so long as they are not
> inspired by the Spirit they remain the word of man.[35]

It might well be disputed whether Bonhoeffer is correct in
so tieing the presence of the Word in the Bible to the interpretation of the Word through preaching. But perhaps at this
point, as in none other in our examination of the relationship

---

33. *Ethics*, p. 260.
34. *The Theology of Dietrich Bonhoeffer*, p. 246.
35. Pp. 160–61; A more detailed discussion of this issue occurs also
in Bonhoeffer's Finkenwalde Lectures on Homiletics.

between Word and human words in the writings of Bonhoeffer, can we most clearly observe the essential role of preaching as a perspective point in the theology of Dietrich Bonhoeffer.[36]

We must now turn our attention to Bonhoeffer's most striking pronouncements, those concerning the church and the world, and ask whether preaching can indeed serve equally both as a unifying concern and a vantage point from which to comprehend these concepts in Bonhoeffer's daring formulations of them.

3

The Church: A Place for Preaching?

On June 8, 1944, Bonhoeffer replied to a letter from Bethge, "Now for your question whether there is any 'room' left for the Church, or whether that room has gone for good. . . . 9th June: I am breaking off here, and will write more tomorrow. . . ."[1] Unfortunately for us, the tomorrow for that question never came, and we are left without the specific reply which we might like.

Nevertheless, countless books and articles by numerous authors have attempted to find at least a general answer to that question from the earlier writings and later letters of Bonhoeffer, particularly with reference to the possible form of the church in the new age. But this issue also is of specific interest to our inquiry as to the role of proclamation as a key

36. GS, IV:11. Even stronger than "perspective point," Bethge uses the word "Richtpunkt"—the point toward which everything aims, and out from which everything moves, if everything else is to be properly aligned.

1. LPP, p. 172.

concept in the theology of Bonhoeffer. If, in fact, our earlier conclusion is correct—that Bonhoeffer saw preaching as the particular locus of the Word of God—then our second question must be, is the church the place in which this proclamation is to take place? And if it has been in the past, will it continue to be in the future?

The Locus of the Word

Bonhoeffer's earlier writings are certainly unequivocal. There can be no doubt that from the beginning of his work the question of the church occupied, or even preoccupied, Bonhoeffer's thinking. In these writings he never leaves the slightest doubt that the purpose of the church, its mission and even its mandate, is the preaching of the gospel. In *The Communion of Saints* he writes:

> The *sanctorum communio,* with the preaching of the Word which it bears and by which it is borne, extends beyond itself and addresses all those who might belong to it, and this is part of its nature. . . . The Church united by the one Word congregates again and again to hear it, or conversely the Word creating the Church continually calls it together anew in a concrete congregation; for it is a Word that is preached, in accordance with God's will and that of the Church, through which he realizes this will. . . . Thus effective preaching is possible only in the *sanctorum communio.* The promise that the Word shall be fruitful applies (Isa. 55:11) to the preaching carried out within the *sanctorum communio.* . . . We do not believe in an invisible church, nor in the kingdom of God existing in the church as *coetus electorum;* but we believe that God has made the actual empirical church, in which the Word and the sacraments are administered, into his community, that it is the Body of Christ, that is the

presence of Christ in the world, and that according to the promise God's Spirit becomes effective in it (pp. 151, 156, 161, 197).

Many other citations from the same work could be listed as well, but these suffice to indicate the unmistakable nature of his emphasis.

Because Bonhoeffer saw concretion as inherent within revelation itself, and because this revelation takes place within the communion of the saints, he could have nothing to do with notions of invisibility with reference to the church. To put his earliest definition of the church in simplest terms, he referred to it as "Christ existing as community." (Fifteen years later, as we shall see, he will define it in terms of "Christ, the man existing for others." But this later expression did not imply a diminution of the significance of preaching in the church, but conversely, an extension of its domain.)

In *The Communion of Saints* he speaks of the office of preaching as having been instituted by the communion of saints itself, and therefore to some extent the preacher is the spokesman of the congregation. Much later, in his *Ethics*, Bonhoeffer moved to insure the priority of proclamation within the community by declaring that "this office is instituted directly by Jesus Christ Himself; it does not derive its legitimation from the will of the congregation but from the will of Jesus Christ. . . . At the same time it is *with* the congregation (p. 259).

In *Act and Being* Bonhoeffer continues his insistence upon the visible church as the community which gathers to hear the preaching of the Word: "The community in question is concretely visible, is the Christian Church which hears and believes the preaching of the Word" (p. 125). This same concept recurs in various formulations throughout *Act and Being*, and in one place Bonhoeffer even asserts that there is no church without preaching ("For church there is none without preaching," p. 143).

But if the church is the body of Christ and the true locus of the Word through preaching, how may all of its many failures be explained, its preoccupation with itself, its confusion and even its godlessness? It should be carefully noted that these sharp questions, so prominent in the last letters of Bonhoeffer, are not ignored even within these earliest works. For example, in *The Communion of Saints* he wrote:

> We believe in the church not as an unattainable ideal, or one which has still to be attained, but as a present reality. What distinguishes Christian thinking from all idealist theories of community is that the Christian community is the church of God in every moment of history and it knows that it will never attain perfection within the development of history. *It will remain impure so long as history exists, and yet in this its actual form it is God's church.* . . . It is precisely in the commonplace surroundings of every day that the church is believed and experienced; it is not in moments of spiritual exaltation, but in the monotony and severity of daily life, and in the regular worship of God that we come to understand the Church's full significance. All else merely veils the true state of things. . . . Until people understand what the church is, and that *in accordance with its nature we believe in it in spite of, or rather because of, all its visible manifestations,* it is not only dangerous but thoroughly unscrupulous and a complete confusion of the Protestant understanding of the church to speak of experiences that can never constitute a Church and in which there is no grasp at all of the church's essential nature (pp. 197–98; author's own italics).

Even in this earliest work Bonhoeffer takes up a crucial theme which he will later reiterate; that is, *that the imperfections of the church as the body of Christ are simply another manifestation of the willing humiliation of the Christ to become flesh and dwell in our midst.*

Similarly, in *Act and Being* he declares that the church can only be a true community because it is "Christ-founded" and that apart from the Holy Spirit within it, it is nothing more than a religious community founded by men and can be observed as "hovering between entity and nonentity" (p. 25). Furthermore, no system of man which is outside of the truth may be allowed to remain, but instead it must be "broken into pieces" in order to make a true system possible. This judgment upon false forms of the church proceeds through preaching: "It is the preaching of the Word that brings about this breakage through faith" (p. 89).

It is obvious that these ideas would lead Bonhoeffer away from a proclamation which is only authorized by the church, and wherein the Word may be captive within the church, to a proclamation which finds its authorization directly from Christ himself and is capable of bringing the necessary corrective judgment upon the forms of the church. This change, as previously noted, takes place in his *Ethics.*

The Cost of Discipleship and *Life Together* continue his emphasis upon the church, although along different lines. In *The Cost of Discipleship,* Bonhoeffer says, "We should think of the church not as an institution, but as a *person,* though of course a person in a unique sense" (p. 185). The church is One Man, the New Man; and the New Man is both Christ and the church. There is a unity between Christ and his church, but nevertheless we must recall Paul's admonition to obedience to Christ as the head of the body. There is therefore no question of a mystical fusion between Christ and his church: "The Church is One Man; it is the body of Christ. But it is also many, a fellowship of members" (p. 187). This body of Christ occupies space on the earth and is therefore visible. In its visible form the body of Christ is the congregation.

How does this body become visible? It does so through its church organization and its life in the world, but particularly through its proclamation. The church becomes visible as the congregation assembles to hear the preaching of the Word of God.

If we would hear his call to follow, we must listen where
he is to be found, that is, in the church, through the
ministry of Word and sacrament. The preaching of the
church and the administration of the sacraments is the
place where Jesus Christ is present. If you would hear
the call of Jesus you need no personal revelation: all you
have to do is to hear the sermon and receive the sacrament,
that is to hear the gospel of Christ crucified and risen. Here
he is, the same Christ whom the disciples encountered,
the same Christ whole and entire. Yes, here he is already,
the glorified, victorious and living Lord. Only he himself
can call us to follow him (pp. 201ff.).

Furthermore, *Life Together* asserts that the assemblage of
Christians in a community of fellowship is a blessing which the
Christian should regard as a rare privilege: "The believer feels
no shame, as though he were still living too much in the flesh,
when he yearns for the physical presence of other Christians.
. . . But if there is so much blessing and joy even in a single
encounter of brother with brother, how inexhaustible are the
riches that open up for those who by God's will are privileged
to live in the daily fellowship of life with other Christians!"
(pp. 19–20).

Some readers of these writings concerning community life,
The Cost of Discipleship, and particularly, *Life Together,* have
concluded that Bonhoeffer saw the answer to the various problems concerning the church in the small group movement rather
than in the gathered church. Anyone who has closely read all
of Bonhoeffer's writings, from *The Communion of Saints* on,
is aware of his extreme reservations concerning these groups.
Not only the Oxford Movement, but also the Volksmission
effort (discussed in his Finkenwalde lectures on homiletics),
and various other attempts at group efforts, aroused the greatest suspicion on the part of Bonhoeffer. Nevertheless, it is
obvious that he also believed in the mutual strengthening and
encouragement of Christians in smaller groups, as his Finkenwalde community specifically represented.

However, it is most definitely not true that *Life Together* was written by Bonhoeffer to describe the only true pattern of Christian living. Godsey has attempted to correct that false impression by translating the brief foreword to that work which was regrettably omitted in the original English translation. Bonhoeffer's aim was clearly set forth in his foreword, which is quoted here in entirety because of its importance:

> An essential characteristic of the subject treated here is that it can be furthered only through joint effort. Because it concerns, not an affair of private groups, but rather a task given to the church, it is likewise not a matter of more or less accidental, individual solutions, but of a common responsibility of the church. The understandable reticence in the handling of this task, which has hardly begun to be grasped, must gradually give way to a readiness in the church to lend assistance. The multiplicity of new forms of community within the church necessitates the watchful cooperation of all responsible people. The following study should not be considered as more than just one contribution to the comprehensive question and possibly also as an aid toward clarification and practice.[2]

In other words, private group efforts do not represent a solution to the problem of the church—particularly not a substitution for the church itself—but only a valuable supplement, and at times, a necessary corrective, to the life of the community as a whole. As such, the church should encourage them, but with a "watchful cooperation," since the matter is not "an affair of private groups" but "a task given to the church."

In his *Christology,* Bonhoeffer continued to locate the Word in the gathered church. He asked the question, "By virtue of what personal structure is Christ present to the church?" His answer: "Christ can never be thought of in his being in him-

2. John D. Godsey, "Reading Bonhoeffer in English Translation: Some Difficulties," *Bonhoeffer in a World Come of Age,* ed. Peter Vorkink, II (Philadelphia: Fortress Press, 1968), p. 121.

self, but only in his relationship to me. That in turn means
that Christ can only be conceived of existentially, viz. in the
community" (p. 47). Again, "Christ is not only present *in*
the word of the Church but also *as* the Word of the Church,
i.e. as the spoken word of preaching. . . . If the whole Christ
is not in the preaching then the church breaks in pieces" (pp.
52–53). Likewise, in an incomplete draft from the year 1942
"Of a proclamation from the pulpit after a political overthrow"
Bonhoeffer wrote:

> God has not forgotten his church. In his unfathomable
> mercy he calls his faithless tormented servants to
> repentance, to a renewal of life according to his holy
> will. . . . In the midst of a Christendom that has been
> smitten with guilt beyond measure the word of the
> forgiveness of all sins through Jesus Christ and the call
> to a new life in obedience to God's holy commandments
> must once more be proclaimed. . . . We call to preaching.
> Proclaim and hear in all places the comfort of the love
> of God in Jesus Christ which forgives sin. Proclaim and
> hear in all places the wholesome commandments of God
> for a new life. Come together to worship as often as
> possible.[3]

A Change of Mind?

Thus in all of Bonhoeffer's earlier writings the church is
identified as a concrete, sociologically describable *place,* as
well as an organism, wherein the Word of God is manifested
through preaching. But what of his later works—his *Ethics,*
and particularly his letters from prison? Did he change his
mind? Did the experiences of the war years, his disillusionment
with the church's compromise and silence, and even with the
helplessness of the Confessing Church, cause him to break

3. *I Have Loved This People,* trans. Keith R. Crim, intro. Hans
Rothfels (Richmond, Va.: John Knox Press, 1965), p. 45.

with his former theology of proclamation? Did he lose confidence in the gathered church, worship, and preaching?

Some have said yes. In his thorough work, *Christ for Us in the Theology of Dietrich Bonhoeffer,* John A. Phillips decided that Bonhoeffer "seems at last to have decided for a nonspacial concretion of the revelation and especially to have refused to continue the development of his past efforts to ground revelation in the visible church." [4] Phillips explains this change as being grounded in Bonhoeffer's "new understanding of the historical situation of the western world"; by which he meant Bonhoeffer's analysis of a world come of age. He particularly bases this conclusion upon the prison letters, where he says there is no more "community of revelation" or "Christ existing as the Church," nor any further "mandates." Instead, revelation is located "in the forms of worldly life." Phillips makes these assertions despite the fact that he admits that Bonhoeffer never answered the question "Is there room left for the church?"

On the other hand, while he does rule out the possibility that the church "might lose its place," Thomas W. Ogletree doubts that Bonhoeffer actually moved in that direction:

> Some of Bonhoeffer's comments suggest the church might at least lose its "place" in the world, its visible existence as an institution. If God himself has been edged out of the world and onto the cross, if he is present conquering power and space in the world only by his weakness and suffering, can the church hope to fare any better? Can it rightfully maintain its "place" in the world if it is to serve such a God? Such an interpretation cannot be ruled out, though Bonhoeffer himself does not seem to draw such a conclusion. He seems to feel that the church will continue to have significance, though perhaps in a radically altered form.[5]

4. (New York: Harper & Row, 1967), p. 142.
5. "The Church's Mission to the World in the Theology of Dietrich Bonhoeffer," *Encounter,* XXV (1964): 466.

Leon Morris feels that Bonhoeffer's own position relative to worship is never made clear. But he was obviously disturbed by some of his statements. He cites Bonhoeffer's remark in one of his letters, "It is remarkable how little I miss going to church. I wonder why." Morris writes, "Evidently he felt little compulsion to worship. And evidently he got little out of worship, else he could not have said that he did not miss it much. . . . It cannot be said that he loved to dwell on the place of worship as did his beloved psalmists." [6]

William Lillie is not so certain that Bonhoeffer had such severe reservations concerning worship, much less that he completely renounced it, but he does feel that Bonhoeffer was wrong in his emphasis upon a time of silence: "About the need of privacy Bonhoeffer was strangely emphatic. There might come again a time when Christians could again openly proclaim their message to the world, but the time for that is not yet. In the meantime, Christ challenges us not to the preaching of the word or even to public worship, but to the living of a worldly life. Bonhoeffer, I think, is wrong here." [7]

Interestingly enough, in *Honest to God,* the book which created much of the furor concerning Bonhoeffer, Bishop John A. T. Robinson writes: "Does this mean he does not want anyone to go to Church or say his prayers? Evidently not. For otherwise he would not ask what was the place of worship and prayer in the absence of religion. For they would obviously have no place." [8] Negatively, however, he says, "This is the essence of the religious perversion, when worship becomes a realm into which to withdraw from the world to 'be with God' —even if it is only in order to receive strength to go back into it. . . . Worship, liturgy, on this understanding, is not meeting the holy *in* the common" (pp. 86–87). Again, "there

6. *The Abolition of Religion; A Study in "Religionless Christianity"* (Chicago: Intervarsity Press, 1964), p. 51.

7. "The Worldliness of Christianity," *Expository Times,* LXXV (February, 1964): 137.

8. (Philadelphia: Westminster Press, 1963), p. 85.

is no sense in which a Christian *has* to turn aside from the world in order to meet God—any more than the Holy of Holies is for him in the sanctuary" (p. 100).

These pronouncements are certainly quite hedged and not as radical as the response of some would lead one to believe, but nevertheless they sufficiently exercised D. T. Niles that he responded, "The Bishop is profoundly wrong." [9] He then followed this remark with a lengthy criticism of the bishop's interpretation of Bonhoeffer's statements on worship, which he regarded as a total misunderstanding of him.

In order to evaluate the conclusions of these writers regarding Bonhoeffer's stance on worship in his later writings, let us briefly cite the pertinent passages from Bonhoeffer's *Ethics* (which must certainly be counted among his "later writings") and his prison letters.

The Mandate of the Church

First, in his *Ethics* Bonhoeffer defines the church: "The Church is nothing but a section of humanity in which Christ has really taken form. . . . The Church is the man in Christ, incarnate, sentenced and awakened to new life. In the first instance, therefore, she has essentially nothing whatever to do with the so-called religious functions of man, but with the whole man in his existence in the world with all its implications. What matters in the Church is not religion but the form of Christ, and its taking form amidst a band of men" (p. 21).

Does the church need "space" in the world; that is, a place for herself? Bonhoeffer replies: "The Church . . . is the place, in other words, the space in the world, at which the reign of Jesus Christ on the whole world is evidenced and proclaimed. . . . She asks for no more space than she needs for

9. *We Know in Part* (Philadelphia: Westminster Press, 1964), p. 141.

the purpose of serving the world by bearing witness to Jesus Christ and to the reconciliation of the world with God through Him." Furthermore, "The Church is the place where testimony and serious thought are given to God's reconciliation of the world with himself in Christ" (p. 68). He is even more specific concerning the question of a "place" for proclamation in the church when he states, "The mandate which is given to the Church is the mandate of proclamation. God desires a place at which His word is repeatedly spoken, expounded, interpreted and disseminated until the end of the world. The word which came from heaven in Jesus Christ desires to return again in the form of human speech. . . . God Himself desires to speak His word in the Church." (p. 259).

A more unequivocal word concerning the relationship of the church to the proclamation of the Word, and the place of the church in the world, can scarcely be imagined.

Bonhoeffer goes on to say that the first demand which is made of the church and those who are members of the church is not that of establishing a religious organization or even leading lives of piety, but "that they shall be witnesses to Jesus Christ before the world" (p. 69). This has profound implications for the church's understanding of her ministry in the world: "Consequently the decisive responsibility of the congregation for the world is always the proclamation of Christ" (p. 289).

There follows next in *Ethics* Bonhoeffer's extensive statement concerning the importance of the office of proclamation to the church, the honor and respect which the congregation should show to it, the true nature of the Bible as the book for preaching, and the dangers inherent in individual interpretations of the Scripture as divorced from the community of faith. Bonhoeffer then flatly states, "The Church as a community is not to be separated from the office of proclamation" (p. 266).

This does not prohibit him from reminding the church of her frequent failures in obedience which have resulted in cheap preaching or "cheap grace"; nor, because of her "exclusive interest in the divine mandate of proclamation," of the failure on the part of the church to discern her own "liturgical poverty and uncertainty of our present day Protestant services, the feebleness of our ecclesiastical organization. . . . This failure has necessarily detracted from the power, the abundance and the fullness of the proclamation itself, because the proclamation finds no fertile soil" (p. 267). Therefore Bonhoeffer describes the church as a fertile field for proclamation.

Again, in Bonhoeffer's discussion of the church and its proclamation, there are warnings abundant, inadequacies and even failures plainly described, challenges for renewal abundantly evident—but again and again there is also the unmistakable identification of the church as the place where the Word of God manifests itself through proclamation.

Does this firm viewpoint alter itself within the prison letters? Admittedly, Bonhoeffer's sharp criticisms of the church reached their pinnacle in these letters and his positive suggestions are minimal, at least in relation to the vast bulk of his other theological writings. But Bonhoeffer himself was aware of this imbalance, and at times even indicated some personal anxiety and discontent with that feature within his work and expressed his impatience to move on to more constructive parts of his work: "Sometimes I am quite shocked at what I say, especially in the first part, which is mainly critical; and so I am looking forward to getting to the more constructive part. But the whole thing has been so little discussed that it often sounds too clumsy. In any case, it can't be printed yet, and it will have to go through the 'purifier' later on" (LPP, p. 208). *It is highly significant to notice that this remark occurs in the last letter in* Letters and Papers from Prison.

Nevertheless, his critical remarks have excited the most attention and are the most often-quoted lines from Bonhoeffer —even if often completely out of their immediate context, not to mention the total context of Bonhoeffer's theological thought. Let us review a few of them which have particular implications for worship and preaching:

December 15, 1943: "By the way, it is remarkable how little I miss going to church. I wonder why" (LPP, p. 91).[10]

April 30, 1944: "The time when people could be told everything by means of words, whether theological or pious, is over, and so is the time that inwardness and conscience—and that means the time of religion in general. . . . How do we speak of God—without religion, i.e. without the temporally conditioned presupposition of metaphysics, inwardness, and so on? How do we speak (or perhaps we cannot now even 'speak' as we used to) in a 'secular' way about 'God'? . . . What is the place of worship and prayer in a religionless situation?" (LPP, p. 139–41).

May, 1944: "Our earlier words are therefore bound to lose their force and cease, and our being Christians today will be limited to two things: prayer and righteous action among men" (LPP, p. 161).

Additional critical citations from the letters might be quoted, but these are the principal ones, and certainly enough to establish that Bonhoeffer posed the most serious questions for the church and its proclamation in the future. In fact, if simply left in their pasted-together form as above, they seem on the surface to have solved the problem of the church's speaking by sweeping it out the door all together.

Two extreme approaches might be taken to these last remarks by Bonhoeffer. On the one hand, it would be possible to dismiss them largely, if not entirely, on the basis of their incom-

10. It may be interesting to notice with reference to this statement a revealing remark made ten days later on Christmas day: "The people here did their best to give me a happy Christmas, but *I was glad to be alone again;* I was surprised at that, and I sometimes wonder how I shall adapt myself to company again after this. You know how I used occasionally to retire to my own room after some great celebration. I am afraid *I must have grown even worse,* for in spite of all my privations *I have come to love solitude.* I very much like to talk with two or three people, but *I detest anything like a large assembly. . . ."* (LPP, p. 102) Furthermore, "I have gotten so used to the silence of solitude by now, that after a short time I long for it again. I cannot imagine myself spending the day as I used to with you, or as you do now." (April 11, 1944, LPP, p. 134).

pleteness and the extreme stress under which they were produced. Bonhoeffer himself might be quoted: "But I wonder whether one's understanding is not affected by the restrictive nature of life here" (June 4, 1943, LPP, p. 34). Or his repeated remark to Bethge that his remarks in these letters were attempts to "clarify his thinking." (See particularly LPP, pp. 139, 145, 184, 200, among others.) The second extreme reaction would be to bind these expressions into a canon of negativism concerning the church, worship, and preaching, a collection of proof texts for previously-held anxieties concerning the present prosperity and the future existence of the church (whether or not Bonhoeffer himself actually shared in these conclusions).

Obviously the more responsible course of action is to set these remarks in the context of other statements made by Bonhoeffer in his *Letters and Papers from Prison,* and then to ask whether this body of literature in fact represents a decisive break with his previous theology, with all of the implications that might have for his conclusions concerning the church and its preaching.

The letters themselves do not yield such an unanimously negative impression on the subject; in fact, when placed in context even his most critical remarks seem to have positive implications for the continuing importance of proclamation as the mandate of the church.

First, let us examine directly several other lines from the letters—many of them, as will be observed, from precisely the same letters as previously cited (italics added by the author):

June 14, 1943: "When the bells rang this morning, I longed to go to church, but instead I did as John did on the island of Patmos, and *had such a splendid service of my own*" (LPP, p. 34).

October 13, 1943: "But in the last resort, for me at any rate, the 'world' consists of a few people whom I should like to see and to be with. . . . If besides that, I could sometimes *hear a good sermon* on Sundays . . . *it would be still better*" (LPP, p. 49).

December 18, 1943: "At midday on Christmas Eve a dear

old man is coming here at his own suggestion to play some Christmas carols on a cornet. But some people with good judgment think it only makes prisoners thoroughly unhappy. . . . And I can well imagine it . . . I think, too, that in view of all the misery that prevails here, anything like a pretty-pretty sentimental reminder of Christmas is out of place. A good personal message, *a sermon, would be better*" (LPP, p. 97).

May, 1944: "Our earlier words are therefore bound to lose their force and cease, and our being Christians today will be limited to two things: prayer and righteous action among men. All Christian thinking, *speaking*, and organizing *must be born anew* out of this prayer and action. . . . It is not for us to prophesy the day (though the day will come) when men will *once more be called on to utter the Word of God* that the world will be changed and renewed by it. It will be a *new language*, perhaps quite nonreligious, but liberating and redeeming—as was Jesus' language; it will shock people and yet *overcome them by its power;* it will be the language of a new righteousness and truth, *proclaiming* God's peace with men and the coming of his kingdom" (LPP, p. 161).

August 3, 1944: "The Church must come out of its stagnation. We must move out again into the open air of *intellectual discussion* with the world, and risk *saying controversial things,* if we are to get down to the serious problems of life" (LPP, p. 200).

Outline for a Book (also on August 3, 1944): *"It* [*the church*] *must tell men* of every calling what it means to live in Christ, to exist for others. . . . It will have to speak of moderation, purity, trust, loyalty. . . . It must not underestimate the importance of human example . . . it is not abstract argument, but example, *that gives its word* emphasis and power. . . . All this is very crude and condensed, but . . . I hope it may be of some help *for the Church's future*" (LPP, p. 204).

August 14, 1944: "God does not give us everything we want, but he does fulfill all his promises, i.e. he remains the Lord of the earth, *he preserves his Church,* constantly renewing our faith" (LPP, p. 206).

How shall this varying witness from Bonhoeffer's last expressions be interpreted? Does Bonhoeffer in fact "leave room" for the church, and in particular for its preaching? By far the larger number of interpreters—including the one to whom these letters were addressed, Eberhard Bethge—are in unanimous agreement that he does.

In the "Editor's Foreword" to *Letters and Papers from Prison,* Bethge wrote, "He sharply criticized his church's centuries old privileges and demand for security, its anxiety about material things, its hierarchical pattern and its juridically constructed doctrines; he broke down its traditional boundary posts—and yet he loved his earthly church to the end" (p. xiii). Later, in his definitive work on the life and thought of Bonhoeffer, Bethge wrote:

> While Bonhoeffer develops his ideas on non-religious interpretation of Christianity in a world come of age, he never considered abandoning for himself his connection with the traditional words and customs of the Church. ... Thus, when he developed his new perspective, he immediately raised the question of what was going to happen to the worship service. This was not in any spirit of breaking it up or, indeed, simply getting rid of it. On the contrary, he was concerned to preserve—as he explicitly states—a "genuine worship." ... It would be a total misunderstanding of Bonhoeffer to imagine that in the realization of his worldly interpretation there would no longer be any community gathered for worship, so that the Word, the Sacrament and the community could be simply replaced by *caritas.* The self-sacrifice of the church in his non-religious interpretation ... is not, then, to be at all associated with the loss of its identity. It is precisely this that is to be re-won.[11]

11. *Dietrich Bonhoeffer,* pp. 784–85. Similarly, "It would be a great mistake to understand Bonhoeffer as abolishing the worshipping church and replacing service and sacrament by charity acts." (Bethge, "The Challenge of Dietrich Bonhoeffer's Life and Theology," p. 35)

Other interpreters have been equally emphatic. Martin E. Marty said, "Bonhoeffer is most seriously misread by students and others when his explorations are taken to mean a denial of Christian community, of the Word and the sacraments. Such a denial would have meant a denial of all his preceding theology." [12] Gerhardt Ebeling also insists that Bonhoeffer's basic "orientation towards the task of proclamation" is never interrupted even in his words of "passionate criticism" toward the church during the time of his imprisonment.[13] He admits that Bonhoeffer's final words in his letters must be taken quite seriously, but "there is surely no overlooking the fact that in the last quotation ['It is not abstract argument, but example, that gives its word emphasis and power.' (LPP, p. 204)] the example presupposes the church's word, and that in the preceeding quotations absolutely everything presses towards the question of proclamation, the coming to expression of the Word of God" (p. 123).

For Ebeling, the crucial question at this point in interpreting Bonhoeffer is grasping the "real theological element at work" in his criticisms of the church: "And that is surely that Bonhoeffer leaves the church utterly and completely to the mercy of what makes the church its true self, and that therefore his theological thinking, too, in order to be rightly oriented towards the church, is oriented towards what makes the church its true self. *That, however, is the Word of God as proclaimed.* This, the foundation of the church's existence, is the criterion of all that is said of the church" (p. 121; author's own italics). All questions concerning the form of the church or of the reorganization of the church, or of the reformation of its worship, must be "connected with the question of proclamation (pp. 121–22).

Likewise Jürgen Moltmann, in taking exception to Bishop Robinson's interpretation of Bonhoeffer, refuses to solve the

12. "Bonhoeffer: Seminarians' Theologian," *Christian Century*, April 20, 1960, p. 469.

13. *Word and Faith*, pp. 120, 121.

riddle of Bonhoeffer's last writings by seeing them as "new, radical departures" from his previous thinking, but rather as "natural developments of his earlier theology"; he finds "hints and suggestions" of his latest thoughts even in his early works.[14] Moltmann insists that Bonhoeffer's later writings do not limit the importance of preaching in the life of the church, but actually extend it when they say that "the office of preaching, as distinct from the Christian life of the congregation, exists to serve Christ's total claim over the world in all spheres of life and not in the church alone" (p. 57).

Pursuing the same track through Bonhoeffer's letters, Eckhard Minthe is convinced that even when Bonhoeffer "ruthlessly exposes" the failure of the church to measure up to the demands made upon it, he is still thoroughly committeed to the church's task and responsibility: "In all this Bonhoeffer's profound concern for the church becomes apparent. . . . They are not a repudiation of the church, not an unofficial declaration of withdrawal or of personal alienation from the church, but a prophetic word that summons to repentance and that looks to the future with confidence in its Lord, a Lord that is still a living Lord in this feeble church." [15]

Finally, James W. Woelfel and John D. Godsey typify the conclusion of many interpreters. Woelfel writes, "The idea that . . . Bonhoeffer set the church to one side is simply without foundation. However problematic the church's forms had become, however radical Bonhoeffer's proposals for its renewal, the Christian community remained to the end of his days at the center of his thought." [16] And Godsey says, "That the notion of Christian worldliness does not dissolve the identity of the church nor exclude its essential functions is easily proved, be-

14. Moltmann, *Two Studies in the Theology of Bonhoeffer,* pp. 15ff.

15. "Bonhoeffer's Influence in Germany," trans. S. MacLean Gilmour, *Andover Newton Quarterly,* New Series, II:1 (September, 1961): 23–24.

16. *Bonhoeffer's Theology: Classical and Revolutionary* (New York: Abingdon Press, 1970), p. 191.

cause Bonhoeffer speaks of its ongoing task of proclaiming the word of God (PFG 140), its secret discipline (PFG 126), its cultus (PFG 179), and its task of intellectual discussion with the world (PFG 177)." [17]

But if these interpreters are correct, and Bonhoeffer does not repudiate preaching as the task of the church, what is to be made of his words concerning silence? Indeed, does not Bonhoeffer say quite plainly, "Our earlier words are therefore bound to lose their force and cease, and our being Christians today will be limited to two things: prayer and righteous action among men" (LPP, p. 161)? In spite of its earlier "mandate" to proclaim, has not the new situation in the world rendered words worse than useless and made deeds our only alternative?

If this is so, then it has far-reaching implications not only for preaching as an act of the church, but for proclamation in the broader sense; and still further, for the nature of worship, the question of the gathered church, and even for the total purpose of the Christian endeavor itself. It is to these questions that we must now turn our attention.

Silence or Speech?

In the face of her own frequent failures in both worship and proclamation, should not the church simply fall silent? Should not deeds replace words, silence replace speech? If not, why not?

Responsible action on the part of the church is always demanded by Bonhoeffer; deeds are essential to make words valid and to empower them. But does he envision a voiceless church as the ideal for Christianity? It is important to see his understanding of the *role* of silence in the life of the church in order not to transform it into an absolutist dogma, a piece of "religion" of its own.

17. *The Theology of Dietrich Bonhoeffer,* p. 271. The pages referred to are from the edition of the prison letters entitled *Prisoner for God* (PFG).

The question of silence is one that had long fascinated Bonhoeffer. In a sermon preached July 15, 1928, in Barcelona, a sermon on Psalm 42:1: "My soul is silent before God, who is my help," (Luther's translation) Bonhoeffer said:

> Our whole being pants for solitude, for silence. For at
> sometime or another we have all tasted what silence is, and
> we have not forgotten the fruit of such hours.... And here
> is the reason why being silent in God's presence requires
> work and practice: it takes daily courage to expose oneself
> to God's Word and to allow oneself to be judged by it, it
> takes daily energy to delight in God's love. But this brings
> us to the question: What shall we do, in order to penetrate
> into this silence before God? Well, about that I can only
> tell you, in all humility, just a little from my own experi-
> ence.... It may be done by taking up a few words from
> the Bible; but the best is to abandon oneself completely
> and let the soul find its way to its Father's house, to its
> home, where it finds rest. And whoever attempts this,
> working at it seriously day by day, will be overwhelmed by
> the riches which will flow from these hours....
>
> Our relationship with God must be practiced, otherwise
> we shall not find the right note, the right word, the right
> language when He comes upon us unawares.[18]

In this early sermon Bonhoeffer stressed the personal values to be gained from silence, the role of silence in hearing the Word, and the relationship of silence to speech.

A similar strong emphasis is laid upon silence, although along different lines, in his *Christology*. In the introduction to that work, he writes:

> Teaching about Christ begins in silence. "Be silent, for
> that is the absolute" (Kierkegaard). This has nothing to do
> with mystical silence which, in its absence of words, is,
> nevertheless, the soul secretly chattering away to itself.

18. Bosanquet, *The Life and Death of Dietrich Bonhoeffer*, pp. 70–71.

The church's silence is silence before the Word. In proclaiming the Word, the church must fall silent before the
inexpressible: Let what cannot be spoken be worshipped
in silence (Cyril of Alexandria). The spoken Word is the
inexpressible: that which cannot be spoken is the Word.
It must be spoken, it is the great battlecry of the Church
(Luther). The church utters it in the world, yet it remains
the inexpressible. To speak of Christ means to keep silent;
to be silent about Christ means to speak. The proclamation
of Christ is the church speaking from a proper silence.
. . . To speak of Christ, then, will be to speak within the
context of the silence of the Church (p. 27).

This passage is of utmost importance in understanding the ex-
tremely paradoxical manner in which Bonhoeffer can speak of
silence and speech. This insight will be of key significance in
properly interpreting Bonhoeffer's later remarks regarding the
church, proclamation, and silence.

Notice that Bonhoeffer's doctrine of silence "has nothing to
do with mystical silence," which he identifies in its absence of
words as "the soul secretly chattering away to itself." The valuable silence which Bonhoeffer urges is the church's "silence before the Word." The church can only have "a proper silence,"
and therefore a proper proclamation, when it humbly waits before the Word and does not "chatter away" in the presence of
the inexpressible. "That which cannot be spoken" is the Word;
nevertheless, "it must be spoken."

In a similar vein, Bonhoeffer says in *Life Together,* "Is there
anything more perilous than speaking God's Word to excess?
But, on the other hand, who wants to be accountable for having
been silent when he should have spoken? How much easier is
ordered speech in the pulpit than this entirely free speech
which is uttered betwixt the responsibility to be silent and the
responsibility to speak!" (p. 104).

In this setting Bonhoeffer is referring to "the ministry of proclaiming," the sharing of Christian speech between brothers.

No one "dares to force himself upon his neighbor" and Bon-hoeffer asks, "Who is entitled to accost and confront his neighbor and talk to him about ultimate matters?" As a matter of fact, Bonhoeffer asserts that the other person has the right to protect himself against such intrusion. Nevertheless, he writes:

> Where Christians live together the time must inevitably come when in some crisis one person will have to declare God's Word and will to another. It is inconceivable that the things that are of utmost importance to each individual should not be spoken by one to another. . . . If we cannot bring ourselves to utter it, we shall have to ask ourselves whether we are not still seeing our brother garbed in his human dignity which we are afraid to touch, and thus forgetting the most important thing, that he, too, no matter how old or highly placed or distinguished he may be, is still a man like us, a sinner in crying need of God's grace. . . . The basis upon which Christians can speak to one another is that each knows the other as a sinner, who, with all his human dignity, is lonely and lost if he is not given help. . . . This recognition gives to our brotherly speech the freedom and candor that it needs (p. 105–6).

Nor may we turn aside from this task of speech in the fear that we shall not be understood, "when we understood very well what was meant when someone spoke God's comfort or God's admonition to us, perhaps in words that were halting and unskilled? Or do we really think there is a single person in this world who does not need either encouragement or admonition?" (p. 106). Fellow Christians share in this mutual responsibility of speaking and listening, and no one should become proud or vain, or else he will be unable either to give or to receive the help which speech can bring. "He has put His Word in our mouth. He wants it to be spoken through us. If we hinder His Word, the blood of the sinning brother will be upon us. If we carry out His Word, God will save our brother through us" (p. 107).

In the same work, Bonhoeffer again related the function of speech to silence, and of silence to the Word: "Silence is nothing else but waiting for God's Word and coming from God's Word with a blessing." Bonhoeffer asserts that this kind of silence is an art that must be practiced and learned, and that real silence only comes as "the sober consequence of spiritual stillness" (p. 79). He warns against an indifferent or negative attitude toward silence which only understands it as a "disparagement of God's revelation in the Word." This kind of negativism toward silence is the result of misinterpreting it as "a mystical desire to get beyond the Word." But this kind of thinking misunderstands the essential relationship between silence and the Word:

> Silence is the simple stillness of the individual under the Word of God. We are silent before hearing the Word because our thoughts are already directed to the Word, as a child is quiet when he enters his father's room. We are silent after hearing the Word because the Word is still speaking and dwelling within us. We are silent at the beginning of the day because God should have the first word, and we are silent before going to sleep because the last word also belongs to God. *We keep silent solely for the sake of the Word,* and therefore not in order to show disregard for the Word but rather to honor and receive it [author's own italics].

Indeed, the final sentence of this quotation is perhaps the key to understanding Bonhoeffer's doctrine of silence in his earliest works and in his latest, most decisive challenges to the church's speech. *Silence is solely for the sake of the Word, to honor it and receive it.*

In his *Ethics,* Bonhoeffer made another important statement on silence as he speaks for the church the words of a confession, a confession of her sins in violating the proper relationship between the Word, speech, and silence:

> The Church confesses that she has not proclaimed often and clearly enough her message of the one God who has revealed Himself for all times in Jesus Christ and who suffers no other gods beside Himself. She confesses her timidity, her evasiveness, her dangerous concessions.
>
> ... She was silent when she should have cried out because the blood of the innocent was crying loud to heaven. She has failed to speak the right word in the right way and at the right time. ...
>
> The Church confesses that she has taken in vain the name of Jesus Christ, for she has been ashamed of this name before the world and she has not striven forcefully enough against the misuse of this name for an evil purpose.
>
> ... She knows that God will not leave unpunished one who takes His name in vain as she does (pp. 48–49).

The obvious import of these words is that the church has been guilty of the sins of speaking when she should have been silent and of being silent when she should have spoken. In both cases, she has taken the name of God in vain. As a result, the Sabbath day has suffered, "because her preaching of Jesus Christ has been feeble and her public worship has been lifeless."

Bonhoeffer's most sharply challenging words concerning silence from his prison letters are well known. But there are other expressions of equal importance which are essential to properly balance Bonhoeffer's views of silence and speech, and these are not so well known. Furthermore, the most radical-appearing of his better known statements take on a renewed significance when viewed in the total context of his previous writings, or even when properly placed within their own context.

In the letter of May 15, 1943, Bonhoeffer felt a great need for conversation with Bethge and expressed it in these words: "If only we could talk to each other about these things. For all my sympathy with the contemplative life, I am not a born Trappist. Of course, a period of enforced silence may be a good thing, and the Roman Catholics say that the most effective expositions of Scripture come from the purely contemplative orders" (LPP, p. 24). In other words, Bonhoeffer could not envision for himself a life of silence.

On November 30, 1943, he returned to the theme of the relationship between speech and the unutterability of the name of God which he had previously formulated in his *Christology:* "It is only when one knows the unutterability of the name of God that one can utter the name of Jesus Christ; it is only when one loves life and the earth so much that without them everything seems to be over that one can believe in the resurrection and a new world; it is only when one submits to God's law that one can speak of grace; and it is only when God's wrath and vengeance are hanging as grim realities over the heads of one's enemies that something of what it means to love and forgive them can touch our hearts" (LPP, p. 86). Here Bonhoeffer asserts that speech is only made possible by the humility of the Christian who recognizes his unworthiness and inadequacy in speech before God. Such a one may find hope, grace, and forgiveness paradoxically present in the threat of life, the submission to love, and the recognition of God's wrath to one's enemies.

But what of those letters where Bonhoeffer explicitly says that the time of words is past, that speech is useless, that the church must learn to live out its witness without such things? Let us examine these statements in their own context, along with other expressions within the very same letters which are often overlooked. Let us then ask what Bonhoeffer seems to have demanded of the church in the way of silence.

The first of these now-famous remarks is in the letter of April 30, 1944: "The time when people can be told everything by means of words, whether theological or pious, is over. . . . How do we speak (or perhaps we cannot now even 'speak' as we used to) in a 'secular' way about 'God'? (LPP, pp. 139, 141). In this same letter, however, Bonhoeffer goes on to say that while he finds it difficult to mention God to religious people, that he was "reluctant" to do so, he could "on occasion mention him by name quite calmly and as a matter of course" to people with no religion at all. His reluctance to speak of God to religious people stemmed from his feeling that it was dishonest, because they conceived of God as the *deus ex machina* which they used to solve their own problems. The inevitable result of this course of action by the "religious" is that God eventually becomes superfluous as man comes of age and is able to solve problems for himself. Therefore Bonhoeffer says, most significantly, "I *should like to speak of God* not on the boundaries but at the center, not in weakness but in strength."

In the letter of May 5, 1944, he writes, "You cannot, as Bultmann supposes, separate God and miracle, but you must be able to interpret *and proclaim both* in a 'nonreligious' sense" (LPP, p. 143).

Bonhoeffer's "Thoughts on the Baptism of D. W. R.," written in May of 1944, contains these challenging words: "Our church, which has been fighting in these years only for its self-preservation, as though that were an end in itself, is incapable of taking the word of reconciliation and redemption to mankind and the world. Our earlier words are therefore bound to lose their force and cease, and our being Christians today will be limited to two things: prayer and righteous action among men." Until the church can purify itself, "the Christian cause will be a silent and hidden affair" (LPP, p. 161). But sandwiched in between these two often-quoted statements is this equally significant remark, quoted earlier: "All Christian thinking, *speaking,* and organizing must be *born anew* out of this prayer and action. . . . It is not for us to prophesy the day (though the day will come) when men will once more be called on to *utter the Word of God* that the world will be changed and renewed by it."

Likewise, there is the tantalizing "Outline for a Book" (August 3, 1944). This brief document has provoked many questions about the church's nature in the future, and in it Bonhoeffer most clearly stresses the church's involvement in the secular. The introduction to this work is often overlooked. This introduction explains the purpose of the whole work: "The

Church must come out of its stagnation. We must move out again into the *open air of intellectual discussion* with the world, and *risk saying controversial things,* if we are to get down to the serious problems of life" (LPP, p. 200). The entire book is obviously concerned about the church's lack of spiritual force, which Bonhoeffer equally accuses pietism, Lutheran orthodoxy, and the Confessing Church of perpetuating; but its purpose was not to stun the church into silence, but rather to move it out of its stagnation into discussion and even into "saying controversial things."

It is obvious that there is much of paradox in Bonhoeffer, and often we do better to leave his words in their dialectic with one another than to attempt a neat systemization which solves all of our problems and eliminates all of their challenge. But perhaps a few conclusions may be profitably drawn from them.

(1) *Speech needs silence.* The church should not always be speaking. In all humility it must recognize the inexpressibility of certain things and the difficulty of verbalization. In its recognition of its own sins of cheap preaching, it must wait patiently for the costly message. It must not believe it has the right to speak equally to all men, in all places, at all times. In silence it must wait *upon* the Word of God, *for* the Word of God, and *after* the Word of God. It must recognize the dependence of speech upon silence: "Right speech comes out of silence, and right silence comes out of speech. . . . One does not exist without the other." [19]

(2) *If the church does not understand the great words of its tradition, and therefore falsifies them, it is better to fall silent.* Whenever the church has become so captive to culture that she declares untruth in the name of the Word; whenever she attempts to blackmail men spiritually on the basis of their boundary needs, rather than challenging them at the very center of their lives; whenever she so misunderstands the Word com-

19. *The Cost of Discipleship,* pp. 58–60. For a discussion of this subject see René Marlé, *Bonhoeffer: The Man and His Work,* trans. Rosemary Sheed (New York: Newman Press, 1967), pp. 83ff.

mitted to her that her pronouncements result in death rather than life—then the church must fall silent and pray until God makes his Word known unto her.[20] (It should be noted at this point, however, that when the church finds itself in such confusion, her actions could not conceivably be more Christlike than her words.)

(3) *Such silence is a sacrifice.* It is not natural for the church to remain silent. Her mandate is proclamation; her mission is the declaration of the Word of God. The Scripture itself desires to be interpreted in proclamation, and the true power of the Word of God desires to break forth through proclamation. Every faithful Christian should pray toward this end. Nevertheless, the faithful Christian will make the sacrifice of silence when necessary and will trust the Holy Spirit to bring on anew the rebirth of proclamation.[21]

(4) *The church must take the risk of speech.* Even though the church must struggle with the problems of "qualified speech" and "qualified silence," it can never ultimately avoid the risk of speech. The church will have to risk bold speech with all of its naïveté, "stammering speech which will be uncertain and incomplete, speech which will prove to be improper and which will therefore have to be discarded in favor of new experimentation." [22] In spite of the difficulty of speaking about God to secular man, it must face an incontrovertible fact, "The biblical faith, unlike Buddhism, . . . must *speak* of God. It cannot withdraw into silence of cryptic aphorisms. A God to whom human words cannot point is not the God of the Bible." [23] So Harvey Cox put it. Interestingly enough, Altizer agrees: "The Christian word is never silent, nor can it be impassive or speech-

---

20. See Ebeling, *Word and Faith*, p. 286, and Bethge, *Dietrich Bonhoeffer*, p. 786.

21. See *Dietrich Bonhoeffer*, pp. 787ff.

22. Phillips, *Christ for Us in the Theology of Dietrich Bonhoeffer*, p. 233.

23. *The Secular City* (New York: Macmillan Co., 1965), p. 241.

less. . . . The word that is silent in our time is a word that has been negated by the World itself. . . . Time is now past when the theologian can be silent in the presence of the moment before him. He must speak to be Christian, and he must speak the word that is present in our flesh." [24]

Nor can there be a substitution of merciful action in the world for the worship of the church in "sermon and sacrament. . . . It is not the intention of Bonhoeffer that henceforth the church should no longer speak of God, Christ, reconciliation, baptism, communion, etc., but only of the world come of age." [25] Indeed, *the very purpose of silence is to make this kind of speech possible. The church can only have the courage to take this risk because it has already acknowledged its humility before the Word,* a humility which leads it again and again into silence. This will be true not only of the gathered church, but also of the scattered church; that is, not only of the church assembled in worship, but the church at work in the world.

But this raises precisely the next question to which we must turn, the question of preaching in relation to worldliness. If, for Bonhoeffer the message of the Word of God is to be found in preaching, and if this preaching is the continuing purpose and mandate of the church—however radically it must purify itself —then how is this to be done in "a world come of age"? How does a proclaiming church relate to a "religionless Christianity"? What does "nonreligious interpretation" mean for preaching?

The crucial nature of these questions is evident, for no matter how closely the Word may be identified with proclamation, and the office of preaching with the mandate of the church, if the world has simply outgrown its need for such things then the era of Christian preaching is ended. On the other hand, is it possible that proclamation itself can serve as the guiding con-

24. Thomas J. J. Altizer and William Hamilton, *Radical Theology and the Death of God* (Indianapolis: Bobbs-Merrill Co., 1966), pp. 138–39.

25. Regin Prenter in *World Come of Age,* ed. Ronald Gregor Smith (Philadelphia: Fortress Press, 1967), pp. 100–1.

cept in uniting the church as its true self with the world in its maturity? "The link between the two entities *church* and *world* is the proclamation of the word."[26]

4

The World: A Need for Preaching?

Bonhoeffer's now famous expressions, "religionless Christianity" or "nonreligious interpretation," and "the world come of age," have been often quoted and thoroughly worked and reworked in theological literature.[1] There is certainly no need to go over this ground again, nor to belabor the point of these issues here. Perhaps, however, a brief summary of their essential significance may serve to positionize us in relation to our more specific inquiry into the role of preaching in a world come of age.

Actually the expression "religionless Christianity" only occurs twice in Bonhoeffer's letters, both uses in his first theological letter from the prison at Tegel, April 30, 1944, at the very beginning of his new approach. Therefore Eberhard Bethge has suggested that it is more appropriate to use the term "nonreligious interpretation," since that phrase or some closely derived expression is used much more frequently by Bonhoeffer in his letters (approximately eleven times). Because "religionless Christianity" was adopted by the English-speaking world so early in the theological writings which discussed his concepts, it must also be mentioned, particularly because of its

26. Bethge, "The Challenge of Dietrich Bonhoeffer's Life and Theology," p. 11.

1. For an examination of Bonhoeffer's use of these terms, see particularly LPP, pp. 139ff., 168–69, 170, 180, 188, 192ff., 200ff., among others.

connection with Bonhoeffer's thinking concerning the subject of "religion" itself.

As for concise definitions of these terms—or perhaps better put, *descriptions,* since "definitions" seems a bit ambitious and actually promises too much—let us look first at "religion," then "religionless Christianity" and "nonreligious interpretation," and finally, "world come of age."

From "Religion" to "World Come of Age"

Religion: As Bethge sees it, "religion" for Bonhoeffer consists of four elements: individualism, metaphysics, a limited sociological province of life, and *deus ex machina;* i.e. the use of God to provide "answers, solutions, protection, and help." [2] To these four might be added a fifth, which William Lillie calls "the most important of all," religion as world renunciation.[3]

Bonhoeffer refers to the "religious premise," by which he seems to refer to the assumption that man can only be appealed to on the basis of his essential weakness before God, and that in fact even his strength is really weakness in disguise.[4] The basic structure of "religion" is the notion that reality must be supplemented by God, a statement which Ebeling takes to be the "common denominator" of the many different things which Bonhoeffer discusses under the term of "religion":

> The thinking in terms of two spheres that is characteristic of religion, striving to make room for God, understanding transcendence in the epistomological and metaphysical

2. Bethge, "The Challenge of Dietrich Bonhoeffer's Life and Theology," pp. 33–34. The term *deus ex machina* (literally, "the god out of the machine") originally stemmed from the Greek stage, where at the crucial moment a god appeared either from a device in the floor, or let down to the stage from the ceiling.

3. Lillie, "The Worldliness of Christianity," p. 134.

4. For a further discussion of this subject, see Anthony J. Wesson, "Bonhoeffer's Use of 'Religion'," *London Quarterly and Holborn Review,* CXCII (January, 1967): 45ff.

sense or in the sense of what surpasses the possibilities of man, localizing the experience of transcendence on the boundaries of existence, treating it schematically as a solution of unsolved problems, God's role as a "stop gap," spying out and exploiting man's weaknesses as proof of his need of God, the view that being a Christian is a special kind of human existence, shifting the emphasis on to an individualistic view of salvation, on to inwardness or into the Beyond, whereby the world is left to its own devices, its godlessness is religiously covered up and God's gifts and his "hours" misjudged.[5]

Taken in this sense, when Bonhoeffer refers to something as "religious" it is scarcely a compliment, but is in actuality a synonym for "the unreal, for pretense, for evasion." [6]

Little needs to be added to these summary evaluations of the concept of "religion" in Bonhoeffer's writings, except perhaps three brief observations. The first is that although these definitions correctly interpret Bonhoeffer's use of the term religion, they also reveal that this is not what the average layman thinks about when he uses the word himself. Therefore some semantic misunderstanding of Bonhoeffer was inevitable—particularly when it becomes apparent that it is also not what some *theologians* understand by "religion," which has resulted in an incredible welter of pronouncements concerning Bonhoeffer's thought on the subject.[7] The second is that while Bonhoeffer admired Karl Barth's contribution to the discussion of "religion," he did not feel that he went far enough and therefore a different perspective must be taken.[8] Third, it should be noted that Bon-

5. *Word and Faith*, pp. 148–50.
6. Dumas, *Dietrich Bonhoeffer: Theologian of Reality*, p. 207.
7. For a discussion of some of these varieties of interpretation, see William Hordern, *New Directions in Theology Today* (Philadelphia: Westminster Press, 1966). In the same place he discusses briefly the difference between Barth's and Bonhoeffer's understanding of "religion."
8. See particularly LPP, pp. 144–45.

hoeffer's attack on "religion" did not first begin during the time of his imprisonment, nor did it leap full grown from the experiences of those days as a kind of disillusionment. It is important that this fact be established in order to prevent the divorcing of his suggestions for "religionless Christianity" from his previous body of theological thought.

In his earliest writings (*Sanctorum Communio* and *Act and Being*) Bonhoeffer's preoccupation with the concrete, material relationship of revelation to the church led him to use the word "religion" as a virtual synonym for faith. In *Sanctorum Communio* he defined religion as "the touching of the human will by the Divine, and the overcoming of the former by the latter with resultant free action." [9]

More specifically, he uses the term positively in this passage from *Act and Being*: "It must be plainly said that within the communion of Christ faith takes shape in religion, and that therefore religion is here called faith, that, as I look on Christ, I may and must say for my consolation 'I believe'. . . . All praying, all searching for God and his Word, all clinging to his promise, all entreaty for his grace, all hoping in the sight of the Cross, all this for reflexion is 'religion,' 'faith-wishfulness' [Barth]" (p. 176). In both of these passages Bonhoeffer can speak of "true religion" in Barth's use of that word; that is, religion transformed and though sinful, "justified" by the revelation of God in Christ.[10]

And yet a one-sided evaluation of Bonhoeffer's use of the term "religion" from this early stage of his thinking would be a mistake. In his earliest preaching, that in Barcelona, he had already begun his incisive criticism of "religion." In these sermons he specifically and categorically denies the identification of faith with religion and continually reiterates the antithesis between them. Bethge says, in fact, that he discovered this theme "anew

9. *The Communion of Saints*, p. 94.
10. For an interesting discussion of this early use of the word "religion" by Bonhoeffer, see Woelfel, *Bonhoeffer's Theology: Classical and Revolutionary*, pp. 126ff.

in every scriptural text." [11] In his very first sermon to the Barcelona congregation he said: "Both the most grandiose and the frailest of all attempts by man to achieve the eternal out of the fear and unrest in his heart—is religion. . . . It is not religion that makes us good in the presence of God, but God alone that makes us good. . . . Religion and morality are the greatest dangers to the understanding of divine grace. . . . We have gradually learnt to understand that with our morality we cannot achieve this, but that religion is part of human flesh, as Luther said."

In a sermon preached on September 9, 1928, on 1 Corinthians 12:9, he said: "What is religion for except to make life more tolerable to man, occasionally to give something to the godly that the ungodly do not have? . . . But what a grievous error, what a fearful distortion of the truth. . . . Thus it is clear that religion does not give us what the world denies us, that religion is not the creator of earthly happiness; no, with religion unhappiness, unrest, become mighty in the world. The antithesis of everything that happens in the world is the word of grace. . . . The cross of Christ destroyed the equation religion equals happiness. . . . With that the difference between Christianity and religions is clear; here is grace, there is happiness, here is the cross, there the crown, here God, there man." [12]

At the same time in an unpublished lecture, "Jesus Christ and the Nature of Christianity," he extended his attack on "religion": "The Christian religion as a religion is not of God. It is on the contrary another example of a mortal road to God like the Buddhist or any other, although of course different in form. Christ is not the bringer of a new religion, but the bringer of God, therefore as an impossible road from man to God the Christian religion stands with other religions; the Christian can do himself no good with his Christianity, for it remains human, all too human, but he lives by the grace of God. . . . So the gift

11. *Dietrich Bonhoeffer*, p. 80.
12. Ibid.

of Christ is not the Christian religion, but the mercy and love of God which culminate in the cross." [13]

This leads us directly to the consideration of the term "religionless Christianity," which perhaps now can be seen more acurately in its historical setting and in its relevance to proclamation in a "world come of age."

Religionless Christianity: Obviously a "religionless Christianity" will be an expression of Christian faith divorced from those elements which comprise Bonhoeffer's understanding of "religion." But what specifically did that mean to him? Eberhard Bethge dislikes the term altogether because of the false impression which it conveys concerning Bonhoeffer's thought. He prefers the term "nonreligious interpretation." [14] In a lecture entitled "The Living God Revealed in This Church" delivered in Coventry Cathedral on October 30, 1967, Bethge said specifically, "The isolated use and handing down of the famous term 'religionless Christianity' has made Bonhoeffer the champion of an undialectical shallow modernism which obscures all that he wanted to tell us about the living God." [15] Bethge was thereby insisting that whatever else "religionless Christianity" might mean, it certainly did not mean that the church would lose her own Christian identity in her task of becoming fully identified with the modern world. Bonhoeffer was as equally concerned with the Christian's identity in the world as with his identification with the world.

John Godsey understands this distinctive identity of a "religionless Christianity" to consist of four elements in the life of the church which would permit it to "most effectively exist for humanity": (1) ecclesiastical self-interest and clerical arrogance would have to be eliminated; (2) the church must learn to live the gospel as well as to preach it, for its example will alone empower its words; (3) it must become the instrument for pro-

13. Bosanquet, *The Life and Death of Dietrich Bonhoeffer*, p. 73.
14. "Bonhoeffer's Christology and His 'Religionless Christianity,'" *Bonhoeffer in a World Come of Age*, pp. 46–47.
15. Quoted in Bosanquet, *The Life and Death of Dietrich Bonhoeffer*, p. 279.

claiming God's Word (albeit in a "nonreligious" language); (4) the Protestant church must regain its own peculiar life, "the proper domain and function of the church as an end in itself" (as Bonhoeffer put it).[16]

Nevertheless, Bonhoeffer's increasingly sharp criticisms of the church in his last letters have prompted many present-day interpreters to translate Bonhoeffer's "religionless Christianity" into "churchless Christianity." Bethge flatly denies that such a conclusion is warranted and says, "But this is a wrong conclusion. Bonhoeffer is quite aware that there must be an ecclesiology if there is to be a Christology, that there are always persons, visibly gathered and drawn into the fate of the Christ person. Christology without ecclesiology is endangered by abstracts." [17] It becomes apparent therefore that "religionless Christianity" has nothing to do with the liquidation of church and ministry, pulpit and altar." [18]

David E. Jenkins echoes these sentiments by stating emphatically "It does no honour to his name and is entirely out of keeping with his life to suppose that 'religionless Christianity' has anything to do with the casting aside of strict spiritual discipline, frequent prayer and the most rigorous attention to the Christian and especially the Biblical tradition." [19] It is in the same vein that Clifford Green writes: "It is perhaps necessary to add that the non-religious interpretation is not a mandate for the rejection of the Church. Certainly Bonhoeffer finds much in the life of the Church that is highly problematical, and he calls for a radical reform. . . . But these are questions about the church's renewal, not its death warrant." [20]

16. *The Theology of Dietrich Bonhoeffer*, p. 273.

17. "Bonhoeffer's Christology and His 'Religionless Christianity,'" pp. 64–65.

18. Theodore O. Wedel, "Man Come of Age," *Union Seminary Quarterly Review*, XVIII (March, 1963): 328.

19. *Guide to the Debate about God* (Philadelphia: Westminster Press, 1966), p. 99.

20. "Bonhoeffer's Concept of Religion," *Union Seminary Quarterly Review*, XIX:1 (November, 1963): 20.

World Come of Age: Finally, Bonhoeffer's expression, "the
world come of age," must be likewise carefully defined, or its
meaning will be totally misunderstood. Bonhoeffer began his
discussion of this term by including within it "the discovery of
the laws by which the world lives and deals with itself in
science, social and political matters, art, ethics, and religion.
. . . Man has learnt to deal with himself in all questions of importance without recourse to the 'working hypothesis' called
'God.' In questions of science, art, and ethics this has become
an understood thing at which one now hardly dares to tilt.
But for the last hundred years or so it has also become increasingly true of religious questions; it is becoming evident
that everything gets along without 'God'—and, in fact, just as
well as before. As in the scientific field, so in human affairs
generally, 'God' is being pushed more and more out of life,
losing more and more ground" (LPP, pp. 167–68). This
"coming of age" continues on the part of the world in spite of
the efforts made by religion to prove that it cannot live "without the tutelage of 'God.' "

Nevertheless, when Bonhoeffer thinks of this maturity of the
world he does not have in mind the conventional "this-worldliness" of conventional secularism: "I don't mean the shallow
and banal this-worldliness of the enlightened, the busy, the com-
fortable, or the lascivious, but the profound this-worldliness,
characterized by discipline and a constant knowledge of death
and resurrection. I think Luther lived a this-worldly life in this
sense" (pp. 192–93). Bonhoeffer best defines his concept of
"this-worldliness" in this same letter of July 21, 1944: "By this-
worldliness I mean living unreservedly in life's duties, problems,
successes and failures, experiences and perplexities. In so doing
we throw ourselves completely into the arms of God, taking seriously, not our own sufferings, but those of God in the world—
watching with Christ in Gethsemane. That I think is faith, that
is *metanoia;* and that is how one becomes a man and a Christian (cf. Jer. 45!)."

This remark makes it apparent that for Bonhoeffer "this-
worldliness" by no means refers to the secularism that is able

to do without God, but to a worldly life which in fact exercises true faith in him, and *as a result enables men to become both truly man and Christian.*

Bonhoeffer does not desire to "gloss over the ungodliness of the world" but to "speak of it in such a way that it is 'thus exposed to an unexpected light'" (p. 191). It is important to observe that Bonhoeffer never equated the world come of age with an optimistic, evolutionary, utopian view of man becoming better and better, although this has been badly misunderstood by some of his interpreters; such as when Fackenheim defines modern man (or rather, has *Bonhoeffer* describing modern man) as "happy in his secularity and free of guilt." [21] Nothing could be more remote from Bonhoeffer's thinking.

Bishop Robinson himself, often the center of the controversy concerning this term, agrees that Bonhoeffer does not mean by "coming of age" that man is "getting better (a prisoner of the Gestapo had few illusions about human nature), but that for good or for ill he is putting the 'religious' world view behind him as childish and prescientific." [22] In this sense, it is "irrelevant and inappropriate" to consider the world as "grown up." [23]

It is precisely this kind of misunderstanding which Paul L. Lehmann acuses William Hamilton of having disseminated in his book *Radical Theology and the Death of God.* Lehmann terms him "the most deliberate and strident disseminator" of a "subtle carelessness" with reference to Bonhoeffer's use of the term "world come of age" and his own understanding of it.[24] Lehmann insists that the proper understanding of Bonhoeffer's

21. "On the Self-Exposure of Faith to the Modern Secular World: Philosophical Reflections in the Light of Jewish Experience," *Daedalus,* XCVI:1, p. 197.

22. John A. T. Robinson, "The Debate Continues," in *The Honest to God Debate,* ed. David L. Edwards (Philadelphia: Westminster Press, 1963), p. 270.

23. Heinrich Ott, *Theology and Preaching,* trans. Harold Knight (Philadelphia: Westminster Press, 1965), p. 13.

24. "Faith and Worldliness in Bonhoeffer's Thought," *Bonhoeffer in a World Come of Age,* ed. Peter Vorkink, II (Philadelphia: Fortress Press, 1968), p. 30.

notion of a world come of age can occur only when the subtle dialectic between identity and identification is maintained: "Bonhoeffer's contribution to a world come of age is his restless and open-ended search for ever new language and ever more concrete ways of keeping the identity of a Christian in the world and the identification of a Christian with the world together" (p. 40).

And as Bethge has pointed out in his extensive biography of Bonhoeffer, this search did not abruptly begin during his days of imprisonment, but can be traced to his earliest sermons and writings, including his preaching in Barcelona, *The Communion of Saints, Life Together,* and *The Cost of Discipleship.* For example, in a sermon in Barcelona on September 23, 1928, he said, "If you desire God, hold fast to the world." [25] This theme is especially taken up in his *Ethics.* That is, from 1937 to 1945 Bonhoeffer was constantly involved with the dialectic between faith and worldliness.

Having thus briefly reviewed various attempts to understand the significance of Bonhoeffer's three most challenging terms, we must now turn to the next question at hand: How can the church speak to the world? What can it do to purify its speech and not falsify the Word? Shall it revise its use of proclamation, its language, its forms? Does the world actually *need* proclamation? If so, what exactly is the importance of preaching in a world come of age?

This key question, the place of preaching in a world come of age, like the more general one concerning worldliness per se, is one with which Bonhoeffer was occupied from his earliest days.[26] It is implicit in all of his questions concerning the church and the world; indeed, he calls it the "link" between

25. Quoted in Bonsanquet, *The Life and Death of Dietrich Bonhoeffer,* p. 70.

26. See Bethge, "Bonhoeffer's Christology and His 'Religionless Christianity,'" in *Bonhoeffer and a World Come of Age,* pp. 46ff.; "The Challenge of Dietrich Bonhoeffer's Life and Theology" in the Chicago Theological Seminary *Register,* p. 8; and finally Bethge again in *Dietrich Bonhoeffer,* throughout, but particularly pp. 60, 78ff., 174ff., 361ff.

both. Two specific questions may serve to suggest, if not an absolute answer, at least a clear direction for the future of preaching in a world come of age. First, *does* the world need preaching, and second, *how* can we speak the Word of God to this world?

Does the World Continue to Need Preaching?

In seeking to answer this question we are most closely directed by the form in which Bonhoeffer himself phrased the concept, "How to claim for Jesus Christ a world that has come of age" (LPP, p. 180). The wording of this question should make two things crystal clear. First, the world come of age does not now stand where it should be, that is, in Christ. Second, this world, with whatever advantages it has derived from its increasing maturity, must nevertheless be claimed for Christ. It is only from this standpoint that we can proceed with any correctness at all to relate the church to the world through the link of proclamation.

Again, when Bonhoeffer says "The question is: Christ and the world that has come of age," he also scores liberal theology for conceding to the world "the right to determine Christ's place in the world; in the conflict between the Church and the world it accepted the comparatively easy terms of peace that the world dictated." He recognizes the contribution of liberal theology in that it "genuinely accepted the battle" and did not attempt to turn the clock back, even though this struggle eventually ended in its own defeat (p. 170).

In this citation, Bonhoeffer makes it clear that the world is not to dictate the terms of Christ's place in the world, and that there is a conflict between the church and the world. In the same letter he criticizes the weaknesses of the pietistic attempts to deal with the world, and even the Confessing Church itself comes in for considerable rebuke. But he does say that by carrying on the "great concepts of Christian theology" the Confessing Church participates in elements of genuine prophecy, among which he lists "the claim to truth, and mercy and of genuine worship." To the extent that the Confessing Church participates in such prophecy it receives attention and *hearing,* even though it is ultimately rejected by the world. But because of a lack of interpretation of these concepts, the force of this prophecy remains "undeveloped and remote" (p. 171).

The world in its maturity has actually come closer to God because it no longer depends upon the sorry "religious" substitutions for the gospel itself—leaning upon a "stopgap" God; being bribed into sociological conformity with the church on the basis of problem solving, boundary threats, and the hope implicit in the *deus-ex-machina.* That does not in any way imply that the confrontation of the world by the church is no longer necessary: "When we speak of God in a 'non-religious' way, we must speak of him in such a way that the godlessness of the world is not in some way concealed but for that very reason revealed rather in, and thus exposed to, an unexpected light" (p. 191). Notice the repeated use of the word "speak," and the necessity for the world to see itself revealed in an "unexpected light."

This emphasis is further strengthened by the exciting letter of July 16, 1944—the very letter in which Bonhoeffer states "God would have us know that we must live as men who manage our lives without him"—in which he goes on to say, "To that extent we may say that the development toward the world's coming of age outlined above, which has done away with a false conception of God, opens up a way of seeing the God of the Bible, who wins power and space in the world by his weakness" (p. 188). Whatever the vantage point the world has gained through its maturity, it only provides it with the opportunity and the necessity of "seeing the God of the Bible."

Nor is the world left to grope along in this direction without any responsibility on the part of the church for proclamation and confrontation:

> I therefore want to start from the premise that God should not be smuggled into some last secret place, but that

we should frankly recognize that the world, and people, have come of age, that we should not run man down in his worldliness, but confront him with God at his strongest point, that we should give up all our clerical tricks, and not regard psychotherapy and existentialist philosophy as God's pioneers. The importunity of all these people is far too unaristocratic for the Word of God to ally itself with them. The Word of God is far removed from this revolt of mistrust, this revolt from below. On the contrary, it reigns (pp. 183–84).

Although it is obvious that it is impertinent, wrongheaded, and ill-advised—not to say, perhaps downright evil—for Christians to "run man down" in his worldliness, he must still be confronted with God. And that, for Bonhoeffer, remains the *continuing* mandate of the church.

In the light of these emphases by Bonhoeffer concerning worldliness and the world come of age, it is inappropriate to adopt any view of the world in its relationship to the church, the gospel, and proclamation, as having "grown up" to the extent that it may live a smug, self-righteous—indeed, "religious"—existence apart from God.[27] Rather, we must see it as "poignant" that mortal man must cope with reality without God: "He is wholly dependent on this world, utterly exposed to the pressure of reality and therewith to its claims. As man come of age he is man given his freedom and thereby summoned in person to the free exercise of his responsibility."[28] William Hordern echoes this theme most succinctly: "In English, at least, 'come of age' has a connotation of maturity; it is a complimentary term. But if Nazism represents a world come of age, we might well seek a way back to childhood. It would seem that Bonhoeffer did not intend the phrase to carry any connotation of praiseworthiness. The German phrase that he used describes one who, having arrived at a certain age, is

27. See Ott, *Theology and Preaching,* p. 13.
28. Ebeling, *Word and Faith,* p. 154. See also Moltmann, *Two Studies in the Theology of Bonhoeffer,* pp. 13ff.

now on his own. He may use his independence for devilish purposes, but he cannot be restricted by returning him to the nursery." [29]

In other words, the world faces a dreadful responsibility as it reaches the age where it may leave the relative security of its nursery-like existence, surrounded by "religion." Thus, along with every individual whose development has led him to the point of individual decision-making, the world lives with the possibility of exercising its newfound freedom for either its own hurt or for its own good. The process is irreversible; and this process of adolescence results in a necessary risk for the world.[30]

To be sure, there are certain rewards, even blessings, which accrue to man because of his maturity. The church must not again fall victim to the mistaken approach of preying upon man's weaknesses or of attempting to convince him that in fact he is miserable even when he is most obviously delighted. The chief blessing which Bonhoeffer sees for the world in its maturity is that it may leave behind its deceptive and sometimes fatally distracting substitutes for the gospel (i.e., its notions of "using" and coercing God, etc.). But man runs the equal risk of "deifying or demonizing" his secularity all over again and turning the blessings of maturity into "a cheap adjustment" to his own culture.

Bonhoeffer must not be understood as projecting a utopian view of man or a progressive view of history, a view he explicitly rejects. On the contrary, if there has been a "clearing of the decks for the God of the Bible," there is also the possibility, as Kenneth Hamilton puts it, of "an empty house waiting for seven more dangerous man-made gods to take the place of the God-of-the-gaps and *deus-ex-machina* that has departed." [31] Compelled now to live with their freedom,

29. *New Directions in Theology Today,* p. 122.
30. See Bethge, "Bonhoeffer's Christology and His 'Religionless Christianity,'" p. 57.
31. *Life in One's Stride* (Grand Rapids: William B. Eerdmans, 1968), p. 60.

men in the world come of age must live without their gods and thus man "can only find the fulfilment of his freedom in bondservice of Christ or drive himself to destruction with ever-increasing speed." [32]

But this negative aspect of the dangers to the world from its own maturity is not the only reason why the church must proclaim the Word of God to it; indeed, it is not even the principal one. Most surprisingly, the true basis upon which the continued proclamation of the church rests is Bonhoeffer's own specific assertion that *worldliness is only possible through proclamation.* In his *Ethics,* he writes: "A life in genuine worldliness is possible only through the proclamation of Christ crucified; true worldly living is not possible or real in contradiction to the proclamation or side by side with it, that is to say, in any kind of autonomy of the secular sphere; it is possible and real only 'in, with, and under' the proclamation of Christ. . . . What is decisive at the present juncture is that a genuine worldliness is possible solely and exclusively on the basis of the proclamation of the cross of Jesus Christ" (p. 263)

Now the true dependence of the world upon proclamation is made perfectly clear. Without the "emancipation by Christ," genuine worldliness is impossible. In its place mankind submits to the rule of "alien laws, ideologies, and idols" (pp. 295–96). Just because it does not hear the preaching of the gospel and allow its life to be liberated by it, the world fails to achieve a genuine and complete worldliness, that is, "allowing the world to be what it really is before God, namely a world in which its godlessness is reconciled with God" (p. 263). What it achieves instead is precisely that from which it has fled, the enslaving domination of a new religion, albeit this time a religion of its own making, a religion which consists in the deification of itself, with a resulting hopeless trust in itself as problem solver. Instead of a *deus-ex-machina,* the world now has a *machina mundi.*

Kenneth Hamilton has expressed this need for the proclama-

32. Daniels Jenkins, *Beyond Religion* (Philadelphia: Westminster Press, 1962), p. 85.

tion of the church as a means of preventing the world from lapsing again into a kind of re-religionizing through its own secularism: "If religionlessness is not absolute, then the Gospel has to be preached to men who are not only estranged from Christian piety but also vulnerable to neo-pagan superstition, not only strongly world-affirming but also despairingly world-weary. The institutional church is required in the world, not because the Gospel is a religious message but precisely because it is the only power that can turn men away from man-made religion. Without the visible Church, the proclamation that God's Kingdom has been brought into the world by Jesus Christ, and will come triumphantly when Christ comes again, will not be heard. Instead, men will fly to salvation-cults when they are fearful; or when they are confident they will deify their own schemes for raising Utopian Babel-towers, and sacrifice their brothers so that their will may be done on earth, even though the whole world must be laid waste in the process." [33]

Bonhoeffer himself said:

> The proclamation of the cross of the atonement is a
> setting free because it leaves behind it the vain attempts
> to deify the world and because it has overcome the
> disunions, tensions and conflicts between the Christian
> element and the secular element. . . . Without or against
> the proclamation of the cross of Christ there can be no
> recognition of the godlessness and godforsakenness of the
> world, but the worldly element will rather seek always to
> satisfy its insatiable longing for its own deification. If,
> however, the worldly element establishes its own law
> side by side with the proclamation of Christ, then it falls
> victim entirely to itself and must in the end set itself
> in the place of God. In both these cases *the worldly
> element ceases to be worldly;* if it is left to its own devices
> the worldly element will not and cannot be merely
> worldly. It strives desperately and convulsively to achieve

33. *Life in One's Stride,* p. 61.

> the deification of the worldly, and the consequence that
> precisely this emphatically and exclusively worldly life
> falls victim to a spurious and incomplete worldliness
> [author's own italics].[34]

Here the paradox of the "exclusively worldly life" which
leads to an "incomplete worldliness" is plainly set forth by
Bonhoeffer, and corresponds with the paradox that true freedom and independence in the world only result from true
discipleship and obedience to Christ. The Christian alone ceases
to be "the man of eternal conflict," but becomes himself an
undivided whole because he professes his faith in both "the
reality of God and the reality of the world; for in Christ he
finds God and the world reconciled." His discipleship is not a
matter of conflict with the world but in fact is the only means
by which man can be truly at home in the world, God's
creature in God's world. "His worldliness does not divide him
from Christ and his Christianity does not divide him from the
world. Belonging wholly to Christ, he stands at the same time
wholly in the world" (p. 67).

Therefore true faith and true worldliness belong together.
This is the only means by which the identity of a Christian in
the world and his identification with the world may be maintained.[35]

In emphasizing the ongoing identity of the Christian faith
as a necessity in its encounters with the secular, Martin Marty
speaks of the Christian as a cousin to the authentic worldling,
"yet a cousin once removed." In referring to some of Bonhoeffer's interpreters who would obliterate this distinction,
Marty said, "Some of his followers had misread his injunction
to erase the line between sacred and secular and to encounter
the godless world, taking him as affirming that such encounter

---

34. *Ethics*, p. 263.

35. For further discussions of this subject, see the articles "Faith and
Worldliness in Bonhoeffer's Thought" by Lehmann and "Bonhoeffer's
Christology and His 'Religionless Christianity'" by Bethge, in *Bonhoeffer
in a World Come of Age*, pp. 25ff. and 46ff.

should be carried on directly. Not at all; I interpret him as saying that the Christian is to the authentic worldling a cousin, yet a cousin once removed. At the crossroads is Jesus Christ, who here represents the suffering participation of God at the center of history, in the cradle and on the cross." [36]

Marty says that direct relations with the world are being established even within the most orthodox and fundamental of American denominations (he says "perhaps most of all there!"). This he sees as scarcely a good thing. It represents no more than a pious aura accompanied by the "wearying eagerness to corner all the beauty queens and all-Americans for each denomination" along with statistical ambitions and the current "fetishistic acceptance of secular norms, external standards, and technical triumphs in church life." It was precisely against such religiosity that Bonhoeffer was protesting and that "both his primitive and his sophisticated readers do well to remember that."

And just as the proclamation of the gospel alone makes possible the true life of worldliness and enables the world to be what it most truly is, so proclamation is the only means for the renewal of the church in its relationship with the world. Just as the world must not take on the form of religion in order to approach Christ, so the church must not take on the form of the world in its life of "being for the world." On the contrary "the church was in the form of the world when it wanted to christianize it by means of the 'religious' interpretation of Christianity." [37] The church is to stand "in the center of the village," and this means that it is to declare its liberating word to all of life; it exists for the sake of the world and stands at the point at which "the whole world ought to be standing; to this extent it serves as deputy for the world and exists for the sake of the world." [38]

36. "Bonhoeffer: Seminarians' Theologian," p. 469.
37. Prenter, "Bonhoeffer and the Young Luther" in *World Come of Age*, p. 175.
38. *Ethics*, p. 266.

In commenting upon this role of proclamation in the church, Moltmann says "The office of preaching, as distinct from the Christian life of the congregation, exists to serve Christ's total claim over the world in all spheres of life and not in the church alone." [39] The church most certainly does not and must not exercise her office of preaching as an excuse for domination over the world, but for the giving of herself in service both to the Word and to the world. Prenter writes, "Put precisely, the world is only of age when it is faced with the church of the cross, and the church is only the church of the cross when it is faced with the world come of age." [40]

But what of the frequent assertion that occasionally and at times the worldly government can so perform its services to the world that the gospel appears unnecessary? If this is true, it would mean that secular institutions do not need the word of the church of Jesus Christ and that secularism can achieve its independent triumph. Bonhoeffer replys that there is never more than

> a limited truth in this observation; genuine worldliness is achieved only through emancipation by Christ. . . . It cannot lead her [the Church] to suppose that this is in itself sufficient, but it must lead her to proclaim the dominion of Christ as the full truth in the midst of all partial truths. When the church perceives that a worldly order is on some few occasions possible without the preaching being heard (but still never without the existence of Jesus Christ), this will not impel her to disregard Christ, but it will elicit from her the full proclamation of the grace of the dominion of Christ. The unknown God will now be preached as the God who is known because He is revealed. [41]

39. *Two Studies in the Theology of Bonhoeffer,* p. 57.
40. "Bonhoeffer and the Young Luther," p. 175.
41. *Ethics,* pp. 295–96.

Here again, the church itself stands in utmost need of the renewing power of true proclamation. Gerhard Ebeling writes concerning the "real theological element at work" in Bonhoeffer's criticisms of the church, "Bonhoeffer leaves the church utterly and completely to the mercy of what makes the church its true self. That, however, is the Word of God as proclaimed. This, the foundation of the church's existence, is the criterion of all that is said of the church." Ebeling identified this as being a question of right proclamation. He acknowledges that it will involve the form of the church, yet "only in so far as the transformation and recasting which Bonhoeffer sees coming to it is connected with the question of proclamation and takes its start from there, so that any premature organization would only mean delaying the coming changes." [42]

The Word of God is therefore indeed the two-edged sword which on the one hand cuts away the "religion" which entangles itself about the feet of the world and prevents its coming to discipleship before God; and on the other hand, it is the sword which pares away all "worldly" forms and endeavors on the part of the church to subjugate the world through unchristian means.

Having examined the "why" of the world's need for preaching (and indeed, also that of the church), we now look at the "how" of that question.

42. *Word and Faith,* pp. 121–22.

5

How Can the Church Speak to the World?

In order to examine this question, we shall have to touch on two further aspects of Bonhoeffer's thought: the "secret discipline," and language renewal.

The Secret Discipline

In his letter of April 30, 1944, Bonhoeffer asks, "What is the place of worship and prayer in a religionless situation? Does the secret discipline . . . take on a new importance here?" Again, on May 5, 1944, he wrote, "There are degrees of knowledge and degrees of significance; that means that a secret discipline must be restored whereby the *mysteries* of the Christian faith are protected against profanation" (LPP, pp. 141, 144).

These phrases present what Paul Lehmann terms "one of the more obscure and problematical of Bonhoeffer's thoughts about the dialectic of identity and identification." [1] Likewise Bethge says that this question has been generally least considered by the interpreters of Bonhoeffer's thought, "for on this subject there has been the greatest uncertainty and also the greatest danger of one-sidedness." [2] But he also affirms the centrality of this question in the context of the larger and

1. "Faith and Worldliness in Bonhoeffer's Thought" in *Bonhoeffer in a World Come of Age*, p. 42.
2. *Dietrich Bonhoeffer*, p. 784.

more determinative question for Bonhoeffer, Who is Christ for us today? It is important although it only occurs twice in the prison letters, and even though Bonhoeffer was never actually able to achieve the satisfactory theological solution to this problem, "much to his own annoyance" (p. 785). It was important to Bonhoeffer because he was concerned to preserve, as he explicitly states, a "genuine worship," and therefore he had no intention of making the church and the world the same thing. "It would be a total misunderstanding of Bonhoeffer to imagine that in the realization of his worldly interpretation there would no longer be any community gathered for worship." The entire question is one of preserving the identity of the Christian faith and at the same time making possible its identification with the world; in this setting, the question of the future nature of the worship service becomes of utmost importance.

The thought itself of an arcane, or secret, discipline originates from the early Christian practice of separating preaching, to which all were invited to attend, from the celebration of communion and the singing of the Nicene Creed, to which only the initiates were allowed. Bonhoeffer seems to be wondering if some sort of return to a similar pattern might not be of profit. It might protect the essential nature of the Christian faith from "profanation." At the same time it might protect the world from a violation by religion through forcing upon it a "cheap gospel," a gospel which is in fact no gospel at all because it is not informed by the Word of God. But since Bonhoeffer never fully developed this concept, nor even defined it precisely, we cannot state categorically what the relationship between preaching and worship would be in this "arcane discipline."

Does Bonhoeffer desire that the church should become completely hidden in her worship and absolutely silent in her preaching, at least for some limited time? William Hamilton and William Lillie both understand the "secret discipline" in this way, although with opposite conclusions, Hamilton with approval and Lillie with disapproval. Hamilton refers to the secret discipline "as a way of witnessing to the ultimate without attempting to call attention to it or give it structure. Both faith and Church are thus utterly hidden, secret, unnoticed." [3] Lillie writes,

> About the need of privacy Bonhoeffer was strangely
> emphatic. There might come again a time when Christians
> could again openly proclaim their message to the world,
> but the time for that is not yet. In the meantime, Christ
> challenges us not to the preaching of the word or even
> to public worship, but to the living of a worldly life.
> Bonhoeffer, I think, is wrong here, for the Christian who
> confines his religious practice to-day to what goes on in
> his own room with the door shut is being just as much a
> hypocrite as the Pharisee who prayed at the street-corner;
> he is living a divided life and that is the essence of
> hypocrisy. [4]

Whatever else Bonhoeffer meant, that is precisely what he did *not* want—"living a divided life." Lillie only understands the occurrence of this concept in Bonhoeffer's thought on the basis of his being biased "by the terrible circumstances of his time." But can it be dismissed on that basis; or indeed, should not the entire matter be understood otherwise? Did Bonhoeffer envision a divided life, a new withdrawal, a retreat on the part of the church?

In exploring this question, André Dumas suggests three possible reasons why Bonhoeffer sought such a secret discipline: (a) either because men cannot understand the language of faith; (b) or because "prayer, suffering and the sacraments are more significant means of expressing the presence of God in the world than, for example, preaching"; (c) or finally, because Bonhoeffer does not feel the time is yet ripe for a new

3. "A Secular Theology for a World Come of Age," *Theology Today*, XVIII:4 (January, 1962): 440.
4. "The Worldliness of Christianity," p. 137.

language purge of its "religious, evasive and pious overtones by the quiet practice, over a sufficiently long period of time, of Christians working in the world?" [5]

Dumas prefers the third answer. He rejects the first alternative because "if that is the case, faith will never find a humanity capable of understanding it, and the secret discipline will always be a sociological presupposition making theological speech impossible." He rejects the second answer because "every difference created here by the secret discipline between preaching and sacrament helps to establish the false notion of an unjustified sacred realm," and he asks, "Why give such a privileged position to prayer and sacramental life to the detriment of the sermon, as though the being of God could never be present except through his Word, the same Word which, to be sure, is prayed, lived, encountered and confirmed in the sacraments, but which is also spoken, announced, secretly heard and publicly proclaimed?"

He recognizes that the alternative which he has chosen makes possible yet a third problem, and that is that "the secret discipline thus runs the risk of enclosing the Word in a questionable kind of secret." But this is not the way Dumas understands Bonhoeffer's meaning, although some have so understood it, because this makes God into "a secret for man to possess." Instead, the secret discipline should "bind the Christian to the secret of God," rather than making God into a secret for man to possess; it should "speak within the incognito" instead of keeping silent and going underground (p. 213).

Bonhoeffer obviously did not mean to drive the Christian back into the very kind of divided life from which the gospel had liberated him; he could not have wished for a new separation into the realms of the "sacred" and "secular." That would be a false hermeneutic of Bonhoeffer, an interpreting of the larger body of thought on the basis of the smaller, more obscure reference. It is equally obvious that he wished for Christians to be disciplined in a private, hidden life which

5. *Dietrich Bonhoeffer: Theologian of Reality*, p. 212.

would nourish them. It would sustain them in those "mysteries" of the Christian revelation which the world cannot understand, a discipline in itself that could not be blatantly advertised and wholesale merchandised to the world.

But in his *Ethics* Bonhoeffer had explicitly stated, "There is no place to which the Christian can withdraw from the world, whether it be outwardly or in the sphere of the inner life" (p. 200). So Bethge concludes, "This means that to understand arcane discipline as a 'place of retreat' would be to deny all that Bonhoeffer intended." [6] In fact, the arcane discipline is nothing other than an extension of Bonhoeffer's lifelong insistence that the Christian should fall silent before the Word until he perceives its meaning for us today. Indeed, this understanding of the Word is not for his own personal edification alone but for its life in the world, to which it was directed and over which it reigns.

In the very letter (May 5, 1944) in which he uses the term "secret discipline" he also says, "In the place of religion there now stands the Church—that is in itself biblical—but the world is in some degree made to depend on itself and left to its own devices, and that is the mistake" (LPP, pp. 144–45). That is precisely what occurs when the church pursues a "positivism of revelation." This is the accusation which he leveled against Barth's thinking. Such an approach takes those doctrines which are "inside doctrines" of the church and cannot be perceived or understood in their true significance by the world (he gives the examples of the virgin birth and the Trinity), shoves these at the world and says in effect, "Like it or lump it."

This would suggest, however, that the silence of the church with reference to its proclamation is not total. The church may have made an error by not perceiving the "degrees of knowledge and degrees of significance" with reference to her doctrines. This may have made her believe that she was ready at all times and in all places to declare all things to all men. Yet

6. *Dietrich Bonhoeffer*, p. 786.

to insist upon total silence from the church in her preaching would make us guilty of an equal error—not perceiving the "degrees of knowledge and degrees of significance" which the Word might sustain in its relationship to the world.

Indeed, in the preceding paragraphs of the same letter, Bonhoeffer had already stated, "You cannot as Bultmann supposes, separate God and miracle, but you must be able to interpret and *proclaim both* in a 'non-religious' sense"; and that "what is above this world, is, in the gospel, intended to exist for this world." In the following paragraph he plainly states that he is "thinking about how we can reinterpret in a 'worldly' sense—in the sense of the Old Testament and of John 1:14— The concepts of repentance, faith, justification, rebirth, and sanctification." The arcane discipline is for reorientation and renewed hearing of the Word, the silence is for reinterpretation.

Therefore the arcane discipline and worldliness are not separate entities but one reality, the reality "of Christ and a Christianity within this world reality." Bethge further says, "We enter the 'sphere' of the arcane in order that there should be an end to spatial barriers. . . . In the *arcanum* Christ takes everyone who really encounters him by the shoulder and turns him round to face his fellow-men and the world. There is no other safeguard against the assertion of two static spheres and the law of a barrier that confers privilege." [7] If the arcane discipline is *not* bound up with the nonreligious interpretation of the gospel in the world come of age, then "arcane discipline in isolation becomes liturgical monkery, and nonreligious interpretation an intellectual game. . . . Arcane discipline without worldliness is a ghetto, and worldliness without arcane discipline is no more than the streets" (p. 788).

Bethge understands the practical significance of this arcane discipline for the church as follows:

> In the *arcanum* there takes place the life events of faith,

7. *Dietrich Bonhoeffer*, p. 787.

praise, thanksgiving and the fellowship of the communion table, and these are not interpreted outwardly.

Christ, the centre of this arcane discipline, continually sends out the "initiated" into their participation in the life of the world, promising them that he encounters and questions them there. They stand shoulder to shoulder with those in their sphere of work and "are there for others." Thus they are waiting for the day when they will also "interpret," not by throwing a religious veil over what already exists, but by creating new life. They can make the sacrifice of being silent and incognito because they trust the Holy Spirit, who knows and brings on the time of the proclamation (p. 788).

There can be no doubt that this interpretation of Bonhoeffer's thought is basically correct, yet it must be asked whether this series of events is in fact linear; i.e., sequentially progressive. Does the church in general now, or at any time, need a special period of days, months, or years when literally speaking she does not speak? Can Bonhoeffer's suggestion be turned into an absolutist dogma, a monolithic, uniform "program" for the church? Would this not in fact insist upon a static relationship between the church and the world at the most intimate level, the very static relationship which Bonhoeffer emphatically denied? Could all Christians, in all times and at all places, in their various relationships with the world, require the same absolute ban upon words at the same time?

If so, then questions must immediately be raised. Can man be man in his wholeness without speech? Can the often-praised realm of "deeds" (as opposed to the often-denigrated realm of "words") be faithfully interpreted by Christians in the world, if indeed their understanding of the Word has become so confused that they are incapable of "taking the word of reconciliation and redemption to mankind and the world"? Finally, can any definition of "deeds" or "living in the world" in fact exclude language; is not language itself an essential part of "deeds"?

Is it not far more likely that this "sacrifice of silence" is a fluid, rather than a static, relationship; that the Holy Spirit will "bring on the time of proclamation" at different times to different members of the Body of Christ in their relationships with the world?

In his interpretation of Bonhoeffer at this point Bethge himself recognized this difficulty: "Bonhoeffer's desire for an 'arcane tact' and a *possible* silence is, of course, *more than can be reasonably asked* of a "Church of the Word" that is *continually speaking.* But what he means is clearly that when the gospel is preached the relationship between God's Word and his world is not an obvious thing and cannot be achieved artificially or by a trick. . . . To *force something* on people is to abandon any hope of its really making a mark on them" (p. 786; author's own italics).

But how, then, if "the church of the Word" is one which by nature must be "continually speaking," is this "possible silence" to be taken seriously? And Bonhoeffer obviously intended it in utmost earnestness. What is the proper relationship between the arcane discipline and the possible silence of the church? When should the church consider silence in its outward pronouncements to the world?

There are at least three situations when the members of the Body of Christ *should* fall silent. (Whether the offending parts will have the insight to do so is another question.) First, the church should fall silent wherever and whenever it has so falsified its witness that it is compromised before the world. Bonhoeffer's remarks specifically occurred during just such a period of the church's existence. The church then has no *right* to speak; it has no *message* from the Word to entitle it to speak; it has no one to *hear* it speak. It *should* fall silent. That it might someday speak. The redeeming word. With power. These things, too, Bonhoeffer said, in the same context. (Notice also that it is a "redeeming" word—no utopian world of a perfected maturity would need redemption.)

Furthermore, the church should fall silent wherever and

whenever its message would be forced upon the world. Bonhoeffer's own hesitation at preaching his last sermon was because of his reticence at forcing the message on some who might not wish it. For the church, this has two practical implications: it will not use sociological conformity to force its message upon the world; and it will not force its "mysteries" (those doctrines which only the initiate can understand) upon the world, saying "Like it or lump it." This protects the innermost truths of the faith from a cheapening before the world and the world from the domination of "religion." The result is interplay between silence and the arcane discipline.

Finally, the church should fall silent when its speech could only be understood as a plea for its own existence. The silence of Jesus before Pilate was just such a silence. "As the lamb is dumb before its shearers, so opened he not his mouth." When its words are no longer perceived as a witness to the Christ but as a preoccupied monologue with itself and its causes as an end in itself, then the church should repent in silence and "bring forth deeds worthy of repentence."

None of this is likely to occur simultaneously by the church as a whole, but rather at different times and at different places, upon some issues or under certain circumstances, by varying parts of the Body of Christ. Bonhoeffer's key concept seems to be that the church that *realizes* its sins and *realizes* that it is being ignored because of them should not cheapen its speech by increasing its volume, or falsify it by increasing its promises. Rather, the chastened church should pray for the revelation of the Word and live the life of faith in the world until its speech can again be heard.

Bonhoeffer's words concerning the "arcane discipline" thus should not be made into an absolute prohibition upon Christian speech, a neo-Trappist withdrawal from the most intimate commerce with the world through the risky subtleties of speech. They most certainly also should not be ignored by a church that is far too glib, far too wordy, far too smugly oblivious to the world's boredom with her garrulous recital of words which have long since lost their intimacy with the Word and her own life among the world. And this, perhaps, is by far the greater danger.

Language Renewal

Implicit in all that Bonhoeffer said concerning proclamation in the world come of age is the question of language. It is also explicit when Bonhoeffer speaks of "the secular interpretation of biblical concepts." "Our earlier words are therefore bound to lose their force and cease." "It will be a new language, perhaps quite nonreligious, but liberating and redeeming—as was Jesus' language; it will shock people and yet overcome them by its power; it will be the language of a new righteousness and truth, proclaiming God's peace with men in the coming of his kingdom." "The time when people could be told everything by means of words, whether theological or pious, is over."

His entire effort toward a "nonreligious interpretation of biblical concepts" was based upon his insistence upon the concrete nature of the Christian message. Therefore William Kuhns can refer to the employment of secular language as *"the* crucial step in the process of eliminating religion." Bonhoeffer's church-world doctrine "implicitly demanded the break from a narrow ecclesiastical vocabulary," which "anticipated a totally secular language for the fundamental Christian truths. . . . There can be no effort made to clarify a Church free of its religious premise without a fundamental overhauling of the language by which that very freedom can be explored." Likewise, "Bonhoeffer believed firmly in the proclamation of a renewed language drawn from the secular world." [8] And Bethge adds, "There is no doubt that Bonhoeffer too is passionately concerned with the contemporary relevance of the kerygma, with the way in which the Gospel can be expressed." [9]

8. *In Pursuit of Dietrich Bonhoeffer* (London: Barnes & Oates, 1967), pp. 202–3.

9. *Dietrich Bonhoeffer,* p. 783.

But the problem of language for Bonhoeffer was far deeper than a question of vocabulary. He was much more concerned with the church's *understanding* of those words, with its means of explaining those words and interpreting them to the world. Something far more significant is required than an artificially adjusted language, so that Bethge also insists, "The invention of new words achieves nothing. This relationship is something Pentecostal" (p. 786).

The essential question does not lie so close to the surface of the matter, so much in the adjustment of the presentation of the message. It has to do again with the key question, Who is Christ for us today? The church must hear the Word and understand plainly that the concreteness so demanded of its proclamation is inherent within the message itself. Concreteness is the attribute of revelation itself. Only with such hearing and understanding will it be able to speak the renewing and transforming word to the world. Therefore Bethge writes: "Do not think now in terms of modernization of the message. Do not think of an attempt to save Christianity by new dressing-up in appearance and vocabulary, by a better translation, by skillful study of speech and sociology of audiences." [10]

There can be no minimizing of the necessity for the understandability of the church's message to the world, and to some extent this certainly presupposes the question of terminology and vocabulary. Ebeling suggests at this point that the criterion of whether our proclamation is understandable should no longer be the believer but the nonbeliever, since this false criterion has resulted "not only in making the proclamation a foreign language, but in also silencing the genuine faith which must repudiate any religious talk that no longer speaks to real man because it does not speak of him." [11] But even this question does not rest upon a popular search for a new "secular" vocabulary which could somehow be heard by secu-

10. "The Challenge of Dietrich Bonhoeffer's Life and Theology," p. 7.
11. *Word and Faith,* pp. 125–26.

lar man, but upon the church's own understanding of its message so that it understands the Word as intimately and concretely involved with the life of the world. So Bethge repeats, "The specific concretion of the message is not a problem of *how* to say what we know anyway but of knowing *what* to say, of knowing *the* message for the day." [12]

The decisive realization for preaching, then, is the knowledge that its message can only be truly relevant, and therefore truly understandable, when it understands the involvement of the Word with the world and speaks of it in that fashion, as Jesus did. Then it will be saved from "religious" language—whether the "language of Zion" or the neolanguage of Zion, the new "in-language" for the new cult.

Preaching in a World Come of Age

Having examined the importance of the secret discipline and language renewal for the future of preaching, we are now ready to look for specific guidelines for preaching in a world come of age.

At first it would seem that at the point of this most pressing and crucial question for proclamation, we find Bonhoeffer's incompleted work at once most tantalizing and most frustrating. Indeed, we seem to be left without any specific guidelines at all. There is, in fact, no concrete program or plan set forth. Bethge says that almost every time Bonhoeffer set about outlining these specifics he was interpreted by bombing raids, and what he wrote later on the subject has been lost. "Thus we are left behind in new territory without his ordinance map to guide us. Or has he perhaps shown us part of the way after all?" [13] A number of interpreters apparently have thought that he did and have attempted to set out, at least partially, the

12. "The Challenge of Dietrich Bonhoeffer's Life and Theology," p. 13.

13. Bethge, *Dietrich Bonhoeffer*, p. 788.

guidelines for future proclamation which Bonhoeffer seemed to suggest.

Bethge has said, "Bonhoeffer has provided pretty decisive categories for evaluating preaching," and listed the guidelines for preaching as he saw them: (1) As Christian proclamation it must avoid the approach of the *deus ex machina.* (2) It must seek to understand the world, and it must allow the people of the world to help give this knowledge. (3) It must not be afraid of ridding itself of religious trappings and philosophical fancy dress. (4) It accepts limitations wherever it has lost its power through its own failures. (5) It will not separate the preached word from the life of the preacher because his life speaks more loudly than his words. (6) The word of renewal can only be spoken by a life which participates in the powerlessness of God in the world. "That is why the congregation must beware of preaching that can be imagined as taking place everywhere, in all circumstances, by anyone to anyone at any time" (p. 789).

René Marlé suggests that Bonhoeffer's work has four implications for preaching. First, it should reproduce, or rather continue, Jesus' call, with all its urgency and actuality; second, it should be aimed at coming to grips with life, to stimulate and thus renew it; third, it should not be content with working out generalities; fourth, it has no meaning unless it is done with authority.[14]

William Kuhns likewise finds four suggestions for preaching, although admitting that a number of others are alluded to: speaking pertinently, nurturing the mysteries of the faith, preparing for a multidimensional life, and rooting the coming church in prayer and action. Ultimately, however, he feels that the most significant guideline toward the essence of the "non-religious interpretation" comes only as the disciple answers for himself the question, "What do we really believe?", and by answering this question is thereby enabled toward interpretation of the faith: "To 'really believe' in the Church,

14. *Bonhoeffer, the Man and His Work,* p. 83.

the word of God, justification, a man must have brought these mysteries into his life and integrated them in the pattern of his values, commitments, and hopes. . . . This concrete interpretation and this ability to insinuate a depth of meaning enable biblical concepts to come alive in a religious interpretation." [15]

In attempting to answer the question "How shall we speak of God to the secular man?", Harvey Cox says that Bonhoeffer gave no answer, but that "from the very issues to which he devoted his life, we may get some hint" and we might "speculate as follows": (1) "A divided church will not speak to the man come of age. . . . Unity is not something for Christians to enjoy among themselves. It is a prerequisite of mission." (2) "A church which eschews politics, or worse still, uses politics to shore up its own position in the world, will never speak to secular man"; (3) "A church whose ethical pronouncements remain generic and abstract will never speak to the secular man." [16]

Some of these answers are tenuous and in the light of Bonhoeffer's total thought, a bit on the surface of things. Others seem to point more directly at the heart of the issues which he raised for the church's proclamation in a world come of age. Are we justified at all at drawing conclusions, however tentative, where Bonhoeffer himself drew none? If so, which elements in his theology guide us toward more specific suggestions in this area?

We must find our answer, if any indeed is to be found, from Bonhoeffer's theology, for his last sermons and interpretations do not reveal any distinctive differences in comparison with his earlier ones that offer evidence of a new method: "The exegesis of the first three commandments of June to July, 1944, like the Pentecost services of 1944 on the texts for the day, speak a language that is no different from before." [17]

15. *In Pursuit of Dietrich Bonhoeffer*, p. 205.
16. "Beyond Bonhoeffer," *Commonweal*, LXXXII (Sept. 17, 1965): 657.
17. Bethge, *Dietrich Bonhoeffer*, p. 789.

Bethge sees this as evidence of how little Bonhoeffer saw the task of proclamation as finding other words for itself, otherwise "Barth's caricature" of Bonhoeffer would be correct: "A little non-religious language from the street, from the newspaper, literature, for the demanding mind from philosophy, is sometimes quite a good thing too for communication . . . even revelation positivism . . . it is understood even by the most remarkable outsiders." But Bethge is convinced that a more careful examination of these exegeses and sermons, along with his earlier ones, leads us to the more convincing conclusion that Bonhoeffer had long since turned toward the world and renounced "religious" language, and that his preaching had been directed along these lines much earlier.

The key question for Bonhoeffer was never the question of knowing *how* to say what we know but of knowing *what to say;* not "how may we better communicate to modern man the message we possess?", but how may we *hear* the Word of God and know *the message* for our day; not how to present Christ to secular man, but "Who is Christ for us today?" Already in 1932 Bonhoeffer had said, "The point is not how are we to model the message, but what really *is* the message and its content?" [18]

The Decisive Clue: Christology

This leads us to look for our guidelines not in catch-phrases, nor even from his suggestions for preaching in his *Finkenwalde Homiletik,* as pertinent and even at points as crucial as they are to these guidelines; but rather in his theology, and more specifically, in his Christology. Here we may find the most significant and helpful suggestions for the church's proclamation in the broadest practical application to the widest number of far-ranging situations. "The proclaimed word is the incarnate Christ himself," and it is "not a medium of expression for something else, something which lies behind it, but rather it is

18. Bethge, "Bonhoeffer's Christology and His 'Religionless Christianity,' " p. 50.

the Christ himself, walking through his congregation as the Word." Therefore whatever is true of Christ must also be true of proclamation.[19] A true theology of proclamation for a world come of age can only come from Christology.

In attempting to answer what Bethge terms Bonhoeffer's "life question," "Who is Christ for us today?", he turns to his new Christological title, "Jesus, the Man for Others." This title fulfills all of the requirements implicit in Bonhoeffer's search for an answer to his life question of Christology, a search which Bethge describes as *humble* because it recognizes that "He is the Christ who is already given." Therefore Bonhoeffer moves with the "humility and certainty of the man who knows whom he is going to meet." [20] The search is *critical,* because the old Christological answers no longer carry the meaning they once expressed. They have instead become obstacles or barriers to the discovery of him. Finally, however, the search is *hopeful,* because Bonhoeffer knew that the challenge of Christ's presence provides promise along with its risks.

Correspondingly, any proclamation of this Christ must contain these same three characteristics. It will be *humble* because it recognizes that *we* are the problem, not Christ. It will not be pessimistic about the presence of Christ in this world and will not waste its time with the weak and pretentious question, "Does modern secular man need Christ?" It will not attempt to reestablish a place for religion in the world, or apologetically seek a sphere for God in either the private or ultimate concerns of man, but it will forthrightly recognize that Christ is already present in his world and that it is evermore up to man to answer the agelong question, "Whom do ye say that I am?"

Second, this preaching will be *critical,* in that it recognizes that endless repetition of its words and its sloganizing have often emptied man's words of the Word and counter-

19. GS, IV: 240.
20. "Bonhoeffer's Christology and His 'Religionless Christianity,' " p. 51.

feited their coinage. Instead of mediating a genuine liberation in the Christ-encounter, our talk has become an impenetrable religious barrier to those to whom Christ would come through his Word.

Third, however—and the church today seems most in danger of forgetting this fact—its preaching must be *hopeful.* Indeed, its true humility toward the Word of God and its critical understanding of its own failures will not lead to discouragement but to hope, and in fact provide the only basis on which hope may arise in that it turns its eyes toward God rather than toward itself. However pessimistic it may be concerning itself, it may be optimistic toward the Christ who is there, in our midst, not only in his Word but in his world; not only judging his church and her words, but liberating and redeeming them; not only rebuking his fallible, stammering servants, but remembering that "a bruised reed he will not break and a smoking flax he will not quench."

Likewise, when preaching comes to understand Christ as "the man for others" it will find that this concept fulfills for preaching, as for Bonhoeffer's Christology, four essential requirements: that of continuity, that of being theological, that of being existential, and that of having ethical implications. That is, for Bonhoeffer no Christology could be adequate which did not maintain *continuity* with the historical tradition; which was not *theological,* expressing something about God more convincing than many of the older and more revered Christological titles; which was not *existential,* making assertions about human existence with a relevance not only for the church but for the world; and finally, which was not *ethical,* thereby prohibiting any flight of man from his specific responsibility relative to God's commandments in the world.

Preaching must likewise positionize itself historically, theologically, existentially, and ethically relative to the Word, the church, and the world. First, it must not seek a self-conscious denial of its *historical* heritage in the church, which inevitably leads to frustration, repression, and a truncated existence; nor may it forget that it proclaims out of an historical given which is based upon the revelation of the acts of God in the Word of God. It must acknowledge that it cannot be biblical without being worldly, but equally that it cannot be worldly without being biblical.

Second, this renewed preaching will have to be *theological,* in that it will not seek a reduction of its message to a self-conscious preoccupation with man, but will confess that the Christ event and the cross stand in the center of life, and that it was only through the incarnation that revelation could reach its height and that God could unite himself with man at the deepest level of communication. Any loss of the profundity of this theological anchorage can only result, and has only resulted, in a corresponding loss of the church's message, in tawdry proselyting and cheap grace, in an utter falsification of the Word either through manipulation of the world or surrender to it.

Third, preaching must also stand in connection with the *existential* since it is dealing with the question "Who is Christ for us *today*?" It must interpret his meaning and confess him before men of our time. (For preaching, Bonhoeffer's ethical dimension is included within the existential, since it is impossible for preaching to be existentially connected with man in the world without equally becoming involved at the ethical dimension.) It must speak to men as Christ spoke to men, with all of the involved concern, earthly involvement and earthy language which Christ himself used. It must see in every *historical* word of God the *existential* involvement with man, not to deify him, but to properly relate him to that Christ who was "Jesus, the man for others."

Finally, and most decisive among the characteristics of his Christology, Bonhoeffer's lifelong answer in preaching and writing to the question "Who is Christ for us today?" was *antispeculative, relational, universal,* and *open.* It was *antispeculative,* because it refused the metaphysical as the determinative category; it was *relational,* because it insisted on the identification of the Christian with other persons as well as upon the identity of the Christian as such; it was *universal,* because with all of its basic involvement with persons and their history Christology nevertheless served as the center point around which everything else gained perspective; and it was *open,* because Christology is fundamentally a never finished task, ever in new response to the encounter with Christ and the world.[21]

For preaching, too, these elements are decisive in the most specific outworkings of practical preaching. It must *avoid the speculation* which robs the Christian message of its inherent concreteness, which loses both outsiders and insiders, the church and the world in a philosophical-speculative haze of metaphysical imagination. It must not "think in a smoke and preach in a cloud" as Spurgeon once put it.

It must be *relational* in the deepest sense, in that it refuses to promote a ghetto-like existence for the Christian in the false hope of "protecting" him from the world or, on the other hand, from "intruding" upon the "domain" of the world. It must be bold in this endeavor, risking as did Christ the accusations of heresy on the part of the religious and "intrusion" on the part of the worldly. It must insist on the authentic world-involvement of the Christian and the church, but it must also never forget the question which should be driving it, as it was driving Bonhoeffer—"How can we claim for Christ a world which has come of age?"

It must be *universal,* in that it places the church in the center of the village and the cross in the center of the church; in that it sees the lordship of Christ not only as a limiting boundary but as the sustaining power of all reality; and in that it recognizes that there is no reality apart from God in Christ and that all reality finds its ultimate unity in him.

And finally, preaching must be *open.* When the last word

21. For a thorough discussion of these and other elements in Bonhoeffer's Christology, see especially Bethge, "Bonhoeffer's Christology and His 'Religionless Christianity,' " pp. 47ff.

has been spoken from the pulpit and the most profound insight expressed, the preacher and his preaching must once again fall silent before the Word, ever waiting in humble expectation to hear what God would have him to know in answer to the ultimate question, "Who is Christ for us today?"

And here the question has come full circle: from the Word, to the church, to the world, to the Word. For preaching, as for Bonhoeffer's thought, that is as it should be. There can be no doubt of the strong demands which this approach makes upon the proclamation of the church. But perhaps, if in some small measure the church may take up his challenge in its preaching, then Bonhoeffer's vision expressed in a sermon of 1932 might be realized: "A proper sermon should be like holding out to a child a shining red apple or to a thirsty man a glass of fresh water and asking: Wouldn't you like it? In this way we should be able to speak about the things of faith so that hands were stretching out faster than we could fill them."

PART TWO

Bonhoeffer's Lectures on Preaching

Introduction

In the tiny Confessing Church seminary at Finkenwalde Bonhoeffer firmly demonstrated the primacy of proclamation in his own life and thought; first, by the place given to preaching in the life of the seminary, and second, by his own personal involvement with preaching and the teaching of preaching. In Bonhoeffer's initial letters explaining the purpose for the founding of the seminary, he clearly stated the important role which preaching and the teaching of homiletics was to play in the life of the community. This practical purpose was specifically carried out in the life of the seminary. Regular worship services, where the students or Bonhoeffer himself preached to one another, as well as practice exercises in the delivery of sermons and Bonhoeffer's subsequent critique of these, shared a prominent place along with meditation and the other theological disciplines taught.

In fact, *listening* to sermons became at least as important an exercise in the life of the community as delivering them or being instructed in homiletics. This condition grew largely out of Bonhoeffer's own deep conviction that the Word of God was present always in preaching, even in the poorest efforts. Bethge says that "even in the poorest attempts from the pulpit, he succeeded in looking for and finding the divine message." [1]

Naturally it was not easy for someone as sensitive and scholarly as Bonhoeffer to educate himself to limit his critical intellect to mere listening, but he did so. In fact, any sermon preached in a true worship service had to be listened to by the group in humility and must not be analyzed. The only sermons he allowed to be discussed were those that were delivered as practice exercises. Only on rare occasions, and then

1. Bonhoeffer, GS, IV:8.

strictly in private, would Bonhoeffer say a word concerning a worship sermon to the preacher who delivered it. Of course there was due attention given to the questions of method and form, but Bonhoeffer's only sharp criticisms were directed toward anything which he regarded as a display of false emotion or a presentation of self rather than the gospel.

This discipline of listening was so significant, in fact, that Bethge suggests that Bonhoeffer's students seemed to be influenced more by his concept of the proper hearing of the sermon than by his methodological suggestions for preaching. Nevertheless, upon the students' own sermonic efforts "nothing exerted so chastening an effect as Bonhoeffer's method of listening to sermons. He himself demonstrated daily what he required in the way of expression, taste, and imaginativeness." Thus, Bethge says, "Homiletics began with the most difficult lesson of all—one's own listening to sermons." [2]

These practical exercises in listening to and delivering sermons were guided by Bonhoeffer's lectures on homiletics. He occasionally entrusted the discussion of sermons to his assistant, but he always reserved the teaching of homiletics for himself. The substance of these lectures was firmly grounded in his Christology. During the first term of the 1935 course Bonhoeffer still saw the sermon as grounded in ecclesiology; that is, preaching exists because the church exists; the sermon has its "causality and its finality" in the church. He did not reject that concept, but in the second course he omitted the lecture based upon it and replaced it with one which asserted that the sermon was grounded in the incarnation: "The Word of the sermon is Christ accepting and bearing human nature. It is not a new incarnation, but the incarnate One who bears the sins of the world." Furthermore, Bonhoeffer followed firmly in Luther's tradition in asserting that there was a sacrament of the Word (*"sacramentus verbi"*).[3]

In spite of this high view of preaching, Bonhoeffer did not set his sights impossibly high with reference to the practice

2. *Dietrich Bonhoeffer,* p. 361.
3. *Dietrich Bonhoeffer,* pp. 362ff.

sermons and thereby intimidate his students. Rather "their confidence grew with every lecture" because of his insistence upon the axiomatic relevance of the Bible. "Do not try to make the Bible relevant. Its relevance is axiomatic. . . . Do not defend God's Word but testify to it. . . . Trust to the Word. It is a ship loaded to the very limits of her capacity."

Bethge says that these lectures were homiletics such as few students elsewhere had the opportunity of hearing, "whether at Berlin or at Halle or at Greifswald." Bonhoeffer's students must have returned changed and happier in their preaching to their congregations. "There can hardly have been one whose confidence and determination did not grow with his knowledge of his ability to do things and demand things of others, and who was not convinced that the freshness of his sermon would depend in large measure upon his view of Scripture as an end in itself and upon his belief in what it presented to him" (pp. 262–63).

True, Bonhoeffer did not at this point have some of the insights which later appear in his prison letters. Bethge says that it was both the strength and weakness of these homiletics that they were so "exactly adapted to the thirties," but that is to be expected in the development of his thought. Nevertheless, these lectures stand squarely in the tradition of his total theology, with echoes to be heard in them and from them in his other writings. They most certainly should not be viewed as an aberrant exception to his "more profound interests," a kind of embarrassing interlude or brief excursion (some might even term it "slumming") into practical theology. For in these lectures, as in Bonhoeffer's life and thought, the "practical" and the "theoretical" are such an integral part of one another that one scarcely knows where the first begins and the other leaves off.

Many of the themes in the following lectures will seem familiar, and indeed they should. From *Sanctorum Communio* to the *Ethics,* and even the prison letters, many of the same themes enunciated in these lectures had already been explicitly stated or would be repeated. This is not to deny, of course, the inevitable modification which occurred in his thought—and indeed, which these lectures themselves reveal as modifications of his earlier thought. Yet those elements presented in his lectures were not isolated themes but a fully integrated part of his earliest and latest thoughts, his concerns, indeed, his practice and life.

For example, these lectures delivered between 1935 and 1939 echo many of the themes already present in his earlier works. In *Sanctorum Communio* he had already presented several ideas which were repeated or amplified in his *Homiletics:* that the Word of God exists in the church in the Bible and in preaching, but essentially in the latter (*Sanctorum,* pp. 160–61); that the authority for the sermon did not reside in the preacher per se (p. 165); that the preaching of the Word may be described in relation to the *sanctorum communio* as that "which it bears and by which it is born" (p. 151); that the Word always creates for itself a congregation (p. 156); that the Holy Spirit may employ even the man who preaches but does not belong to the *sanctorum communio* (pp. 162–63); and finally, he expressed his fear of experience or experiences as a replacement for faith (p. 198).

In *Act and Being* he had previously stated other themes which occurred again in these lectures: in the preaching of the Word of God there should be no note of uncertainty (p. 142); the Word must judge all subjective, untrue thought systems (p. 89); revelation takes place within the church through preaching (p. 122); dogma is not the aim but the condition of preaching (p. 144); the preacher himself must recognize that "at this very moment, in this very place, through his very self, Christ wishes to address the communion" through the sermon (p. 147).

Likewise, in his *Christology,* Bonhoeffer asserted that while Christ himself was present *in* the proclamation, and therefore "the proclaimed Christ is the real Christ," nevertheless "this proclamation is not a second incarnation" (p. 46); the imperfections of proclamation are a part of the new humiliation of Christ in his incarnation (p. 47); preaching should be accorded a prominent place, and this place "belongs to even the simplest preaching" (p. 52); Christ is present in the church as the spoken Word, "not as music and not as art" (p. 53); proclamation, as a sacrament, does not stand as a symbol for something else, it does not *mean* something, it *is* something (p. 55); in spite of the difficulties of interpretation which arise from "the concealment in history" of God in the Bible, nevertheless "the risen One encounters us right through the Bible" (p. 76). All of these concepts are repeated in various forms in the *Homiletics*.

In his lecture delivered in Gland, Switzerland, in 1933, entitled "The Church Is Dead," Bonhoeffer scored the pastors and theologians for their indifference to the Scripture and their neglect of the reading of the Bible, even as he would later do in his *Homiletics:* "We are more fond of our own thoughts than of the Bible. We no longer read the Bible seriously. . . ." (*No Rusty Swords,* p. 185).

The interplay of Bonhoeffer's thoughts is also evident in the works which were written at approximately the same time as his lectures on preaching, *The Cost of Discipleship* (1937) and *Life Together* (1939). In *The Cost of Discipleship* Bonhoeffer had already stated that there is no mystical fusion between Christ and his church, in spite of the fact that Christ is present in the church as the Word (p. 187), and that the church becomes visible as it assembles to hear preaching. In *Life Together,* a number of themes present in the *Homiletics* had already been presented: the evangelical preacher must learn the Bible for himself and be able to give scriptural "proof" (p. 55); the reading of Scripture is comparable to the reading to others of a letter from a friend—it should demonstrate both the proper distance and the proper interest (p. 56); the preacher must not ask how he is going to preach on a text, "but what it is saying quite directly to him" (p. 82); the preacher must wait in patient meditation upon the Word until it becomes clear what God's Word to us is (p. 82); it is not necessary for the preacher to discover either new ideas or extraordinary experiences in his meditation, but he should allow the Word to dwell within him even as Mary "pondered in her heart" the things that were told to her (p. 83); false authority is based upon personalities rather than upon the Word of God (p. 109).

Likewise many of the themes set forth in his *Homiletics* were later repeated by Bonhoeffer in his *Ethics:* the primary purpose (or in the *Ethics,* the "mandate") of the church is proclamation (pp. 76ff.); the duty of the preacher is to prepare the way for the Word (pp. 92–93); the preacher must not impede the movement of the Word to the congregation (pp. 96–97); it is the duty of the Christians to assemble for worship: "It is an essential characteristic of the divine revelation through the Word that I must go to hear it preached if I am to hear this Word at all. . . . If the Word is to be able to come to me, then the last act in the preparation of the way, the last deed in the penultimate, is that I go to the place at which it has pleased God to impart his Word." (p. 97); "the Word which came from heaven and Jesus Christ desires to return again in the form of human speech" (p. 259), and "what the church proclaims is the word of the revelation of God in Jesus Christ" (p. 259); the Scripture desires to be interpreted and preached, and this is its truest nature (p. 260); there is no legitimate proclamation by the church which is not a proclamation of Christ (p. 261); wherever Jesus Christ is proclaimed there is always the congregation (p. 265); the church as a community is not to be separated from the office of proclamation (p. 266).

During his imprisonment Bonhoeffer saw a number of his insights being worked out in human history, and he looked forward to the day when preaching, as he understood it in his theology of proclamation, should once again come to its true place. His prison letters reveal an ongoing concern with the question of proclamation: the church had become incapable of taking the word of reconciliation to the world through her preoccupation with herself (p. 161); it is the Word of God that shall someday renew and change the world, and men will once more be called on to utter it (p. 161); because the Word has not yet been properly apprehended, there must come a time of silent waiting upon it (pp. 161–62); the Word of God must not make its confrontation with the world from below, (i.e., from psychotherapy and existentialist philosophy) because the Word of God reigns (p. 184); one's subjective presence in a community enables the preacher to understand how Christ is "formed" in it (p. 186); when we speak of God we must not conceal the godlessness of the world but reveal it, even when we speak of God in a "nonreligious" way (p. 191); the proclamation of the gospel must risk saying controversial things (p. 200).

Perhaps more significant than these scattered references, some of which sustain a tenuous connection, at least directly, with the lectures on homiletics, is Bethge's general summation of the total import of these letters with reference to Bonhoeffer's evaluation of the importance of preaching: "It is a misunderstanding to use his last expressions to make him the chief witness against preaching. To preach often not only appeared meaningful to him, it was his most certain reality in the face of death." [4] Bethge insists that for Bonhoeffer, "discipleship, suffering, silence, worldliness—all that does not take the place of the sermon, but serves for its enthronement" (p. 9). His concern for the sermon "was not a matter of fearfulness," but of confidence in the ultimate value of the sermon. "The 'secular interpretation of biblical concepts' does not mean the discontinuation of preaching, but the first step toward its renewal for the world" (p. 12). Surely these statements stand fully in the spirit of the Finkenwalde *Lectures on Homiletics.*

In addition to the many similarities between Bonhoeffer's earlier works and his *Homiletics,* these lectures provide their own unique contribution to Bonhoeffer's thought. They cannot be said to constitute his last word upon the role of preaching as the link between the church and the world, but nonetheless

4. Bonhoeffer, GS, IV:7.

they represent an important word, and one that deserves far more attention than it has yet been accorded.[5]

Of course there are the many practical sections which will interest the preacher and homiletician. These include discussions on the use of the Bible and the relation of the text to the sermon; the place of teaching in the sermon ("There is teaching in the gospel, but the gospel is not teaching"); the construction of the sermon, involving the question of the central point of a text and the development of outlines; the relationship between the writing of the sermon and the use of notes; the delivery of the sermon, including a fascinating and at times amusing discussion of the various deliveries produced by varying theologies, and the interesting insight that the true place of birth for the sermon is the pulpit, not the study; his words concerning true emotion and his warnings against emotionalism; and finally, perhaps most practical and interesting of all, his concluding rules for evaluating sermons and his list of sources of error in preaching.

Of wider interest to the general student of Bonhoeffer's thought will be his discussions regarding the separation of preaching from the sacraments and the creed in the early church; the connection between the incarnation and the proclaimed Word; the fascinating section on the meaning of being a witness; his significant statement on the relation between the church, ordination, and preaching; the significant addition to his previous thinking concerning the subject of the concretion of the Christian message, in his "Excursus" which deals with the event of concretion in preaching; his discussion of the relation between meditation and proclamation; his interesting comments about the Oxford Movement and small groups; and finally, his detailed examination of subjectivity and objectivity, both true and false, in proclamation.

The following lectures do not, therefore, provide us with

5. It is surprising how little known the work is in either German or American theological circles. In my own reading I have only discovered two references to it in English language literature and three references in German literature, none extensive.

a curious sidelight but a direct insight into the most fundamental of Bonhoeffer's concerns: the proclamation of the Word
of God.[6]

Historical Considerations

The New Testament contains several expressions for preaching:
*kerussein, euaggelizein, esthai, didaskein, marturein, pres-
beuein,* each with its own distinctive emphasis. *Kerussein* refers to public proclamation, such as the announcements of an
ancient herald on a foreign assignment. It suggests an element of newness, the announcing of something which has
not been heard before. *Euaggelizein* expresses more strongly
its connection with the subject matter of proclamation, with
the joyful content of the message, the *euaggelion.* Its simi-
larity to the word *aggelos,* or messenger, underscores the element of mission in the message and indicates that one allows
himself to become the bearer of good news. It is in this
spirit that the preacher should enter the pulpit, as the messenger from Marathon with his exultant cry—"The victory is
won!" *Didaskein* and *didache* suggest the content of the message, the clear facts of the case, the report of something worth

6. Lectures delivered each semester between 1935 and 1939 [as-
sembled by the editor (E. Bethge) from transcripts of various courses
during this period. The following abbreviations indicate when each
particular section of the lecture was originally delivered or transcribed:
S.S. = Summer semester, W.S. = Winter semester.

This reconstruction of the original lectures is based upon transcripts
from J. Kanitz and E. Bethge (S.S. 1935), W. Koch (W.S. 1935/36),
G. Riemer (S.S. 1936), J. Mickley (W.S. 1936/37), O. Dudzus and
K. Vosberg (S.S. 1937), H. W. Jensen (W.S. 1938/39). The original
copy of Bonhoeffer's lectures no longer exists.]

knowing. *Kerussein* and *euaggelizethai* are related to the mission sermon or to evangelistic preaching. *Didaskein* connotes the building up of an existing congregation through daily instruction in previously unknown doctrine. *Marturein* and *marturia* suggest the testimony of Jesus before Pilate, as well as the testimony of Timothy before many witnesses. These two words connote the closest possible relationship between the proclamation and its proclaimer; in other words, that as I preach, I allow myself to become a witness for something else, something outside of myself—but nevertheless that the witness which I give is also my own, my personal testimony. In these words the distinction between ministry and person is the least suggested. This concept is found often in Acts and in the pastoral Epistles, in which the separation of ministry and person moves completely into the background. "Perform your ministry, that you may be saved" (1 Tim. 4:16). Only in one place, 2 Tim. 2:9, is the separation noticeable. Reformation theology differs somewhat in this respect.

Omilein in the New Testament does not refer to public preaching but rather to speaking confidentially with one another. (For example, the conversation of the disciples at Emmaus, Luke 24:14–15; 1 Cor. 15:33.) Only later, in the seventeenth century, did this expression come to be the designation for the science of preaching [homiletics].

Besides the public *kerygma,* private assembly of Christians in homes was practiced in early Christianity (Acts 2:46, and in other places). In these small circles the actual practice of preaching to a congregation began. The first evidence for such services stems from Justin Martyr. After the reading of a text (probably the *lectio continua*), an elder of the congregation addressed a short exhortation to the gathered congregation. This exhortation later became the homily, which had the purpose of warning the congregation against false teachings. The first preserved homily is known as the Second Epistle of Clement. The homily then became an exposition of Scripture in connection with the reading of a text, and thus the sermon was born. By the time of Origen the homily was no longer a speech before a closed circle of Christians, but cata-cumens and heathen as well were allowed to attend this part of the assembly. But under Origen, however, the "secret disci-pline" also began; that is, the holding of a private meeting to receive the sacraments, and to recite the confession of faith (the creed) and the Lord's Prayer (the *Pater Noster*). This closed meeting was begun to provide protection for the church against the mockery of the world. The sermon then became separated from this inner worship service; it was conducted publicly so that catacumens and heathen could attend. It should be noticed, however, that in the New Testament the possi-bility of the admittance of the heathen to preaching was already considered (1 Cor. 14:23).

After the time of Origen the simple sermon developed into the artistic homily, that is, into synthetic sermon arrangement or theme-preaching. The thematic sermon is one in which a subject is set forth as well as a text; as, for example, in the early sermons concerning Mary, the great saints, or specific matters of interest to the congregation. Examples of thematic preaching are to be found in the preaching of the Church Fathers (in the library of the Church Fathers, *Köselche Kirchenväter*).

Preaching has the dual objectives of establishing the Chris-tian congregation and building it up. In the early centuries the separation of believers and unbelievers in worship was clear and meaningful, and this division at first did not present any particular problem for these objectives of preaching. The matter first became problematical under Constantine and with the development of the mission, or evangelistic, sermon. Even today we are still occupied with the proper connection be-tween the missionary and congregational character of the ser-mon. Schleiermacher saw the sermon as an expression of the religious self-awareness of the preacher and a presentation of the pious convictions of the congregation, as if there really were such; he consciously ignored any empirical evidence. The Church of England has lost hundreds of thousands of members to the Methodists because it no longer paid attention to these dual objectives of preaching, or else no longer distinguished between them, and quit evangelizing [*nichtmehr missionerte*] —or perhaps because it only taught in its preaching and presupposed a mindset in the congregation that was not there.

Our question now is how we may come to the proper kind of sermon, one in which both the establishment and the building up of the congregation may be accomplished, one in which *kerussein, didaskein, euaggelizethai,* and *marturein* may be realized and kept in proper relationship to one another.

[*W.S. 1935/36–1937*] 2

The Proclaimed Word

1. The proclaimed word [*Predigtwort*] has its origin in the incarnation of Jesus Christ. It neither originates from a truth once perceived nor from personal experience. It is not the reproduction of a specific set of feelings. Nor is the word of the sermon the outward form for the substance which lies behind it. The proclaimed word is the incarnate Christ himself. As little as the incarnation is the outward shape of God, just so little does the proclaimed word present the outward form of a reality; rather, it is the thing itself. The preached Christ is both the Historical One and the Present One. (Kähler: the preached Christ is the so-called historical Jesus.) He is the access to the historical Jesus. Therefore the proclaimed word is not a medium of expression for something else, something which lies behind it, but rather it is the Christ himself walking through his congregation as the Word.

2. In the incarnation the Word became flesh. God, the Son, took on human form. So he accepts all of mankind and bears it in himself, in that he is fleshly [*indem er Fleisch tragt*]. He embraces the whole of humanity with its genuinely sinful nature. That he wears this humanness is the whole mystery of

the Gospels. It is not enough to say that he suffers with man-kind—he actually takes mankind upon himself. It is false to say that the Logos accepted, that is, adopted, man; instead, he has taken on human nature, my nature and your nature. His flesh is our flesh and our flesh is his flesh. This also means that in the incarnation the new mankind is established. Man-kind has become one through the incarnation. The congrega-tion is already present in the Embodied Christ; his body is "we ourselves." The church is included in the incarnation as the *sanctorum communio*.

3. The proclaimed word is the Christ bearing human nature. This word is no new incarnation, but the Incarnate One who bears the sins of the world. Through the Holy Spirit this word becomes the actualization of his acceptance and sustenance. The word of the sermon intends to accept mankind, nothing else. It wants to bear the whole of human nature. In the congregation all sins should be cast upon the Word. Preach-ing must be so done that the hearer places all of his needs, cares, fears, and sins upon the Word. The Word accepts all of these things. When preaching is done in this way, it is the proclamation of Christ. This proclamation of the Christ does not regard its primary responsibility to be giving advice, arousing emotions, or stimulating the will—it will do these things, too—but its intention is to sustain us. The Word is there that burdens might be laid upon it. We are all borne up by the word of Christ. Because it does so, it creates fellowship. Because the Word includes us into itself, it makes of us members of the body of Christ. As such we share in the responsibility of upholding one another. Thus the word of Christ also presupposes Christian brotherhood. The Word in-tends that no one should remain alone, for in him no one re-mains alone. The Word makes individuals part of one body.

4. Word and congregation. Because the word conveys the new humanity, by its very nature it is always directed toward the congregation. It seeks community, it needs community, because it is already laden with humanity. At this point it is significant to notice that the word produces its own momentum.

It proceeds from itself toward the congregation in order to sustain it. The preacher does not therefore accomplish the application of the word; he is not the one who shapes it and forms it to suit the congregation. With the introduction of the biblical word the text begins moving among the congregation. Likewise the word arises out of the Bible, takes shape as the sermon, and enters into the congregation in order to bear it up. This self-movement of the word to the congregation should not be hindered by the preacher, but rather he should acknowledge it. He should not allow his own efforts to get in its way. If we attempt to give impetus to the word, then it becomes distorted into words of instruction or education or experience. As such it can no longer uphold the congregation nor sustain it. Upon Christ, however, who is the proclaimed Word, should fall all of the need, the sin and death of the congregation.

5. The form of the proclaimed word. The form of the preached word is different from every other form of speech. Other speeches are structured so that they have some truth which they wish to communicate either behind them or beneath them or over them, or else they are arranged so as to express an emotion or teach a concept. These human words communicate something else besides what they are of themselves. They become means to an end. The meaning of the proclaimed word, however, does not lie outside of itself; it is the thing itself. It does not transmit anything else, it does not express anything else, it has no external objectives—rather, it communicates that it is itself: the historical Jesus Christ, who bears humanity upon himself with all of its sorrows and its guilt. The sustaining Christ is the dimension of the preached word. The biblical content of the proclaimed word makes clear this distinction from all other forms of speech. Cultic expressions only make it unclear. How can our words again become the proclaimed word in this original sense?

6. The unique dignity of the word. The promise to be able to accept men and sustain them has been given to the spoken word. Nothing is equal in dignity to the spoken word. As the

Logos has adopted human nature, so the spoken word actualizes our adoption. It is *that* word which the Logos honors, not some magical transaction. Therefore our adoption is not a matter of some kind of psychi-magical act through which we are adopted and included into Christ. What really happens is that we are accepted through the clearly heard and understood word of Christ. Cult and liturgy can therefore only serve as adoration, celebration, and praise of the clearly spoken word of God. Proclamation, therefore, in the strictest sense, does not issue from cultic ritual but from the testimony of the word. Liturgy and cultic acts serve proclamation. In the proclaimed word, according to the promise, Christ enters into his congregation which in its liturgy adores him, calls unto him, and awaits him. In the proclaimed word Christ is alive as the Word of the Father. In the proclaimed word he receives the congregation unto himself. Through the Word the world was created. The Word became incarnate. The incarnate Word continues to exist for us in the Scripture. Through the Holy Spirit, the incarnate Word comes to us from the Scripture in the sermon. And it is one and the same Word: the Word of creation, the Word of the incarnation, the Word of the Holy Scripture, the Word of the sermon. It is the creating, accepting, and reconciling Word of God, for whose sake the world exists.

7. Because we were created by the Word and are daily kept by it, because we have been reconciled through the Word before we knew it, therefore only through this Word are we able to recognize God. Through this Word we find certainty. This Word alone affects our will. Only this Word keeps on being clear to us in its accusations and its promises. Only this Word makes us without excuse. Music and symbols (as the Berneuchen movement believed) do not make us without excuse; they are not unequivocal and do not break down the will! Music and symbols do not create the *anthropos pneumatikos,* but likely the *pseukikos.* The word, however, conveys the Spirit and does accomplish this. With cultic endeavors we are in danger of wanting to add something to the preached word, of attempting to lend a particular style of expression to it.

But it may not be and does not need to be so undergirded. The word of the sermon is not one species of the genus "word," but rather it is just the opposite: all of our words are species of the one, original Word of God which both creates and sustains the world.

For the sake of the proclaimed word the world exists with all of its words. In the sermon the foundation for a new world is laid. Here the original word becomes audible. There is no evading or getting away from the spoken word of the sermon, nothing releases us from the necessity of this witness, not even cult or liturgy. Everything revolves about the accepting and sustaining witness of Christ. This is the way we must learn to look at the sermon again.

8. While the Word accepts and sustains us, there is nevertheless no fusion of God's being with ours, no identification of the godly nature with human nature. The Word accepts us and bears us in that he forgives sin and keeps us in the commandments of God. The relationship of the Word to us is one of providing forgiveness and assurance along the pathways of our lives. There is no mystical metamorphosis which occurs, but rather faith and sanctification.

9. The sacrament of the word (*Sacramentum verbi*). Because the Word is the Christ accepting men, it is full of grace but also full of judgment. Either we will let ourselves be accepted and be forgiven and be borne up by Christ, or we remain unaccepted. If we ignore the spoken word of the sermon, then we ignore the living Christ. There is a sacrament of the word.

10. Therefore the preacher needs to approach the sermon with the utmost certainty. The word of Scripture is certain, clear, and plain. The preacher should be assured that Christ enters the congregation through those words which he proclaims from the Scripture. Luther could say that the preacher did not have to pray the fifth request of the Lord's Prayer after his sermon ["Forgive us our trespasses"]. The sermon should not leave the preacher despairing and perplexed, but rather it should make him joyful and certain.

The Witnesses

1. "You shall be my witnesses" (Acts 1:8; Luke 24:48).[1] The disciples said of themselves "Whereof we are witnesses" (Acts 2:32); "We have seen and bear witness" (1 John 1:2; 4:14; 5:11). To be a witness, *marturein,* means: (a) to acknowledge and manifest what one has seen; (b) the obligatory statement before a court, upon which life itself can hang. A person does not cause himself to be a witness. He becomes an eyewitness to something and is called upon by others to be a witness. It is the good pleasure of God to call the apostles to be witnesses.

2. The apostles are witnesses because God is the first witness (1 John 5:9; Rom. 1:9; 1 Thess. 2:5; Phil. 1:8); because Christ is a witness (Rev. 1:5; 3:14); because the Holy Spirit is a witness (1 John 5:6). God manifests that which is true and thereby comes under the judgment of men. Christ gave testimony to a "good confession before Pontius Pilate" (1 Tim. 6:13). The Holy Spirit testifies to the truth of the witness concerning Jesus Christ. In a testimony, the one who testifies guarantees his word, and therefore under certain circumstances he has to suffer for it. Christ represents God before the world and suffers for it. The Holy Spirit is witness to that.

3. What do the apostles do as witnesses? They bear witness of the testimony of Christ; that is, witness of the one in whom word and deed converge. They do not bear this witness of themselves, but from him. Their word is therefore a witness

1. In the small church at Flossenburg, Germany, the town in which Bonhoeffer was hanged, there is a tablet with this inscription: "Dietrich Bonhoeffer, a witness of Jesus Christ among his brethren. . ."

only because it has the testimony of God and of Jesus as its subject, and because they are honored to be witnesses of the resurrection. So they are neither witnesses through their own worthiness nor through their suffering. *Marturein* originally was not identical with the concept of dying as a witness. One's own death is not witness of itself but in the strictest sense a testifying to the suffering of Christ. Only later there came a shift in the meaning. *Martus* then meant one who dies, in distinction to one who confesses. Originally a witness became a witness through the preaching of the death of Jesus. The apostles were the chosen eyewitnesses of that event. They had "seen and touched," but this was not the result of their worthiness. For this witness, of course, they had to involve their own lives—that is a part of it. Their own experience was nevertheless not the witness itself.

4. How can we be witnesses? Must we also have "seen and touched"? Must we have had experiences with Jesus and testify to these? Must our actions be added to our preaching and support our testimony? Schreiner says that only through word and deed is a testimony given. To the preached word belongs the acting of the church. (H. Schreiner "Die Verkündigung des Wortes Gottes," Schwerin 1936, pages 117ff.) Here Schreiner parallels the New Testament. Word and deed were a unity in the life of Christ. We have to be witnesses to this unity. But there occurs a falsification of the testimony if we think we have to add something to this witness through our experience. The apostles did not do so either.

5. Our sermon is a testimony based upon the witness of the apostles. Theirs is based upon the testimony of Christ. We do not testify to what we have seen and touched, but to what they have seen and touched. We declare the biblical testimony as faithful witnesses (Rev. 2:13). The biblical testimony is the testimony of Christ who is the faithful witness (Rev. 1:5).

6. Conclusions:

(a) Our speech is not a spontaneous witness, but commissioned by and bound by the biblical witness. It does not spring from our own private interests or initiative. Its content is the biblical witness alone. Christ will honor this kind of witness.

(b) If the sermon is to be a witness, it must be a testimony of Christ. Only where Christ is preached is God present. Without him the sermon is at best nothing more than empty doctrine. If Christ is preached, then the sermon is a witness. The witness of Christ involves both preacher and listener in word and deed. That does not mean that there is something else which has to be added to it by the hearer, but that through listening with our whole being we either testify to or deny the witness.

(c) As a witness to Christ, the sermon is a struggle with demons. Every sermon must overcome Satan. Every sermon fights a battle. But this does not occur through the dramatic efforts of the preacher. It happens only through the proclamation of the One who has trodden upon the head of the devil. We usually do not recognize Satan anyway. We do not find him; Christ finds him. The devil departs from him. Satan waits nowhere so for his prey as where the congregation gathers itself. Nothing is more important to him than to hinder Christ's coming to the congregation. Therefore Christ must be preached.

(d) If our preaching is to be a testimony to the biblical witness, then we must have a reverence for the biblical word. For the apostles are the faithful chosen witnesses. The word does not belong to us, it is Christ's. It pleased Christ to reveal himself through the biblical texts, and therefore we should not make the text a springboard for our own thoughts. Contempt and disregard for the biblical text hinders the coming of the Christ and makes the *marturia* impossible.

(e) The witness wishes to stand behind his testimony. He does not want to add anything with human words to Christ's words. He is not to dominate, but Christ. He lives under the discipline of a witness. Therefore he does not want his hearers to look at his life and regard it as a prop for his testimony. Of course his witness will surely be hindered if the speaker does not allow himself to be disciplined by the word and his life to be directed by it. The witness can easily make his words unworthy of belief. But he does not want to, and indeed may not, cite his own accomplishment as the confirmation of his testimony. As he preaches, the witness himself is continually involved in the decision for or against the preached Christ.

[1935–1939] 4

The Ministry of Preaching and Ordination

What significance do ordination and the office of preaching have for the sermon? The preached word is commissioned to the office of preaching. This task is invested with promise. The ministry of preaching and the office of the pastor are not identical, even as today the Word of God and our sermons are not identical. The ministry of preaching constitutes the church's ministry rather than the office of pastor. The ministry of preaching is intrinsic and remains as such; the office of pastor is a specialized division of the preaching ministry. It may be taken from us. Its form should be adapted to the preaching ministry. Ordination is the call to a preaching ministry and not primarily to the office of pastor. The commission to preach continues to be mine even if I am separated from the pastoral task within a congregation. Ordination is the conveyance of the ministry of preaching by the church in general, while the installation into a specific pastoral office is a particular act. This is the Lutheran understanding of ordination in contrast to the Reformed church concept in which a person is ordained to the pastorate of a particular congregation. The ministry of preaching is an enduring commission from which a person cannot free himself after ordination.

The confessional writings speak of ordination as a "possible" sacrament (Apology XIII, 11). In fact it seems difficult to understand why it should not be a sacrament. It has the mandate of Christ with the giving of the keys; it has the outward sign in the laying on of hands; it is an action of the church invested with promise. Nevertheless, ordination is not numbered among the sacraments. A sacrament conveys a saving grace to the one who receives it. But that is not the case in ordination. Ordination does not convey the gift of the forgiving of sins to the one who receives it, but rather the specific commission to proclaim forgiveness.

The Word comes of its own accord and intends that it be proclaimed. So the church remains a servant of the preached word, even if the present form of our preaching as a pastoral, publicly-allowed matter, with its usual liturgical and methodological form, is lacking at this time. The Word comes, and the ordained man cannot again detach himself from the service of a witness; only the church can do that. The ministry of preaching is no independent trade.

This ministry of preaching is characterized by its word, its commission, and its certainty. Besides the word and the external commission, what else can indicate a certainty of a call? The New Testament recognizes a permissible desire toward the "excellent" ministry (1 Tim. 3:1). This desire should be sincere. In this sense there is something like an inner certainty of call to the preaching ministry. Ordination and this certainty belong together. In reality they are often widely separated from one another. There is ordination without subjective certainty of calling, just as on the other hand there is a certainty of call to witness without ordination. And in reality the promise of the preaching office depends upon the *ordinatio* and not on the subjective certainty. In ordination this promise becomes applied. If therefore ordination gains greater authority than the subjective certainty of a call, that nevertheless does not mean that the proclamation of the unordained is without promise. We must only say this: No one is to demand ordination without the certainty of a call. That simply is not done, just as one should not receive the sacraments without faith.

Actually the one who is uncertain as he is ordained does not lose the promise as he enters his ministry. But the word that is commissioned to him and that should sustain his congregation, and in fact by which he will not allow himself to be sustained—this word will overwhelm him. He will only get to sense the curse of his office and not its blessing. His ministry will bring him to judgment. The destruction of his ministry may take many forms. Either he will be overcome by an unchristlike absence of peace, which will result in an attempt to certify his ministry through unholy, restless church work; or he will abandon himself to the so-called objectivity of the word in a resigned inactivity. Both are destructive, evidence of his not being able to bear the commission, because his certainty is lacking.

What is the subjective certainty of a call? It is the knowledge that one is absolutely and totally unworthy of call, and that in view of one's own faith such a call is completely unjustified. Whoever feels himself cut out for the ministry is already lacking its first requirement. The certainty of call has nothing to do with pride, or with a personal security and conceit which says, "The Lord needs me." Luther began his pulpit prayer in this way: "Lord, I am not worthy . . . but because the people need your teaching. . . ." Besides these negations, however, positively said there should be a real love for the ministry, the congregation, the gospel. Love for the ministry involves also its commission.

In the Methodist church it is the practice for the congregation to appoint someone to the ministry before his formal training and to delegate him to the study of theology. But it is nevertheless permissible to desire this office. In 1 Timothy 3:1 the office of a bishop is called a *kalon ergon*. Truly it should be not a boring work, but a pleasant one, to serve the congregation of Christ. It is true that there are certain conditions imposed, such as that the called one should be *didaktikos* (1 Tim. 3:2), but where a great love for the ministry is lacking there soon arises aimlessness and boredom, indeed, a disgust with this work. This love, which in fact is a love for the gospel, will express itself in daily life, in prayer, and in Bible reading. And when all of this comes under attack and is about to fall apart, even then we cannot go back and get loose from our responsibility to testify for Christ. The temptation to give up the ministry will pursue us. But that is no measurement of our worthiness. The ministry will never turn loose of us again. And Isaiah 6 is true: the one whose sins are forgiven is ready for service.

[*S.S. 1935–S.S. 1936*] 5

The Causality and Finality of Preaching

How does my word become the preached word, Christ's word? What content, what form should it have? This is the question of the "where from" (the source) and the "where to" (the object) of the sermon.

1. The source of the preached word is not the pious Christian experience or consciousness of the preacher, nor the need of the hour of the congregation, nor the desire to improve and influence others. All of these things quickly collapse and lead to resignation. These motivations and forces are not enough. The only valid source of the sermon is the commission of Christ to proclaim the gospel, and also the knowledge that this commission comes to us from an already existing church. The source of the sermon is nothing other than the existence of the church of Christ.

The authority and the content of the sermon are determined by this fact. The authority of my particular world-view and the force of its inspiration is not sufficient; the authority of the commission alone is sufficient. Neither the authority of the experiences of a prophet nor the authority of some crying religious need is a valid authority; Christ's commission alone has validity. The contemporary situation is not sufficient to determine the content of the sermon; the dealings of God with men as they are testified to in the Bible and made known through the teachings of the church is sufficient.

2. For what purpose do I preach? The preacher should have something he wants to accomplish through his sermon. But it may be that the preacher for that very reason may spoil the essential thing if he sets out to ask, into what frame of mind do I intend to bring the people? What do I want? As with Schleiermacher, to declare the pious consciousness of the congregation? To build up the congregation, to inspire them, to teach them? To convert the people?

The issue may not be settled in that way. Everything hinges on the question of what the gospel is. Is it inspiration, education, conversion? Certainly it includes all of these things, but all under the one goal that the congregation of Christ might become the church. I preach, because the church is there—and I preach, that the church might be there. Church preaches to church. This means that I do not set a personal goal for myself to pursue, a goal of either inspiration or edification.

I must refuse to indulge in tricks and techniques, both the emotional ones and the rhetorical ones. I must not become pedantic and schoolmasterish, nor begging, entreating, urging. I do not try to make the sermon into a work of art. I do not become unctuous and self-centered or loud and boastful. By forsaking my personal ambitions I accompany the text along its own way into the congregation and thus remain natural, balanced, compassionate, and factual. This permits the Word's almost magnetic relationship to its congregation. I do not give life to it, but it gives life to me and to the congregation. The movement of the Word to its congregation is accomplished through the interpretation of it.

It is characteristic of this kind of preaching that the preacher will not exhaust himself. The preacher should not fully exhaust himself and physically push himself to the limits. Whenever that happens there is always too much subjectivity in play. Here we are not talking about a weaker subjective participation on my part, but about a completely different kind of participation, a humble awareness of the Word and a belief in the power of the Word itself to make its own way.

A certain distance must remain between the actual subject of the Word and myself. In texts of wrath, for example, I am not the one who is angry. God is. God converts, not I. It is as if I read a letter which another has written. I report factually what another says. It is really a higher degree of participation which allows one's own subjectivity to die. It is scarcely the right situation when applause is handed out for a sermon according to the mental agility of the speaker. When the sermon is regarded as an interpretation, then the involvement of the preacher is that of a man who puts himself to death for the sake of the Word, who dies to his own will and only wishes to be a handservant of God. He wants only what the Word itself wants.

3. This causality and finality (both basically identical in significance) signified that the church preaches only *one* sermon in all of its messages, and this sermon is not dependent upon current events and their circumstances. It is *one* truth to which the church testifies. This truth is not the result of deductions; it is not the communication of a certain body of doctrine. It is truth that has taken place. It creates its own form of existence. It is possible for the church to preach pure doctrine that is nonetheless untrue. The truthfulness of it hinges upon the form of manifestation which the church adopts for itself. This form, however, implies discipleship and not proximity to what people expect or unity with their culture. It is not the church which suits the people, but the church which is obedient that is heard. This form of existence does not simply mean that we do the same things that others do, except that we do them a little better, but that we do things differently.

The basis of the preaching church is not flesh and blood,

customs and culture [*Blut und Boden*], and its form is not one of cultural unity, but rather its basis is the Word and its form is obedience. To attempt to get close to the culture of the people and to the contemporary scene is actually to get separated from both the contemporary and the people. All of that sort of thing is highly foreign to the church. The contemporary truth of the church is revealed in that it preaches and lives the Sermon on the Mount and the admonitions of Paul. The credibility of the Christian message is not strengthened by looking for so-called "people-pleasing" means which are actually foreign to it.

The church also causes its ministry to be condemned when it does not live in the truth which it proclaims. There is a great danger that is connected with all auxiliary aids to worship, and that is that the preacher will seek to create a congregation of one sort or the other according to some already predetermined image. But he is not to create an image for the congregation, and certainly not a congregation according to his own image. In fact he has no idea at all how it should look. God himself creates his congregation. The face of the congregation should not be determined according to some kind of ideal for a congregation; God engraves his signs in other ways than I imagine. The pious preacher should be particularly aware of this fact.

Excursus: The Factor of Concreteness in Proclamation

1. The sermon is concrete only when God's word is really in it. God alone is the *concretissimum*.[1]

2. It has pleased God to speak to us through the words of the Bible. Therefore the sermon must be an interpretation and not an application. Every application on our part indicates that we stand above the Word rather than beneath it; that we regard it as a principle which has to be applied to each individual case. The only true application, however, is God himself, and he alone. The maximum of concreteness which we can achieve is through factual exposition of his Word. It is

1. A discussion following the lecture, S.S. 1935.

God's call to acknowledge his lordship, and beyond that there is nothing more concrete.

3. Which texts are concrete? Basically, every text. It is the one and the same God who speaks in every word of Scripture. We start with the supposition that the one God witnesses to himself as well in Romans 13 as in Acts 5:29 or Matthew 5–7. The selection of a text is relatively unimportant from the standpoint of concreteness. According to Luther, the whole of Scripture is unanimous and clear. This is not a statement which is the result of examining every text, it is a presupposition. If we regard the Scripture as ambiguous, then we treat it as a varying collection of commands and admonitions and not as a testimony of God. We are therefore freed from the necessity of locating and quantitatively sorting out which texts fit our times with the least ambiguity. We are not to seek a text to suit the times. The ambiguity of the Scripture is the mark of its servanthood which God uses to speak his unanimous Word and to make himself revealed. The ambiguity of the Scripture can be overcome only by the Scripture itself and by nothing else.

4. Can the preacher have an authoritative, concrete word for a concrete situation? God alone is concrete. Each admonition, however specifically concrete, must not have as its final purpose the proclamation of the admonition itself, but of God. He is the Giver and the Lord of the admonition. The final question is not *what* has validity, but *who* has validity. The admonition as such is nothing. Otherwise we create men according to our ideals, instead of leaving God room to create his own likeness in man.

5. The so-called concrete historical situation is ambiguous. Both God and the devil are at work in it. It cannot become the source of our understanding and proclamation of the Word of God. The concrete situation is the situation to which the Word of God speaks. It is the object of concretion, not its subject. It is also not the criterion by which concreteness can be measured. The Bible, in its canonical form, is the criterion. (Is the devil also in the Bible? The Bible is in any event also a piece of

"historical situation," with all of the consequences of that. People have attempted to protect themselves from this frightening realization by the doctrine of inspiration. In order to do so, the Bible has been taken out of its historical situation. A re-developed doctrine of inspiration might say that God reveals himself in spite of all of the failures of the words spoken by men, and that he turns his Word back unto himself. But in such a statement there lies the real danger of a new substantiation of the doctrine of inspiration.)

6. The true concrete situation is not the historical one, but rather the situation of the sinner before God who wants to assure himself before God and with God. The answer to this true concrete situation is the crucified and resurrected Christ who calls us to faith and discipleship. That the crucified Christ lives is evidence that the real concrete situation of man is the one which came to light A.D. 30.

6

The Pastor and the Bible

1. The pastor encounters the Bible in three situations: in the pulpit, in his study, and in the place of prayer. In all three places he must be careful to use it properly. But he has to struggle to do so. The Bible is a grossly neglected book with pastors. "Forgive us our trespasses" in this, too! To win this battle for the proper use of the Scripture is the best possible theology. A Protestant must become mature in his use of the Bible.

2. The pastor only uses the Bible properly when he uses it totally, that is, in this three-fold sense. There cannot be one use without the other. No one can interpret the Bible from the pulpit who has not dealt with it in his study and in prayer.

3. The Scripture in the pulpit. This is its most proper use.

The Scripture is intended to be interpreted through proclamation in order that it might go forth into the life of the congregation. The preacher is only its servant and helper [*Handlager*, lit., "handy-man"]. He does not bring it into the pulpit for his own use; he allows himself to be used by it for the congregation. He entrusts everything to the scriptural word. He should want this Word to enter into the congregation in order that the members might become mature in its use. That is his task as an evangel.

4. The Scripture in the study. The pastor must know what he is dealing with when he takes the Scripture into his hands. He becomes involved with the perception of truth. Therefore he will have to take into consideration the following presuppositions:

(a) The Bible is that book in which God's word is stored until the end of all things. In this it is different from all other books. This presupposition cannot be ignored in any work done with the Bible.

(b) For two thousand years the church has gained knowledge of the truth from this book. We are not the first ones to read this book correctly. Liberal theology has not always been able to protect itself from this kind of pride. The Reformation and the old church are more powerful interpreters than we are.

(c) This book has comforted millions and led them to God. Probably every word in it has had a part in doing so and has its own piece of history in Christianity. Criticism should guard itself from becoming a too-easy offense to the congregation.

(d) A knowledge of the Scripture should not lead to glory and pride. A humble mind is better than a clever mind. We study the Scripture representatively for the congregation of Christ. We do it to be able to preach it and to pray about it better. A hurried, hasty reading of the Scripture is inappropriate and unworthy of it. It is essential that we have a basic and comprehensive knowledge of the Scripture. That is the teaching of the Church Fathers, Augustine, Luther, and the reformers. That is the teaching of our grandfathers. Luther read the Old Testament twice a year, the New Testament more often. The study of the Scripture should be reserved for the best time of day, just as the time of prayer should be. A knowledge of the Scripture is essential for our work among the congregation—not only for the sermon, but for the death bed, for the sick, for the tempted, for the desperate, and for the proud. In the work of pastoral care the devil himself moves against us. We cannot oppose him with anything else but the Word.

A knowledge of the Scripture must also serve to provide us with those theological theories which we publicly advocate. We must be able to prove the Scriptures. That puts us on solid ground. Otherwise we establish theories on the basis of our life experience and not on the Word. Sensational stories do not establish any truth. The decisive arguments for the church come from the Scripture. From it we must be able to give answer for our decisions on church polity and for every action taken by the councils, the examining commissions, and the seminaries. The time comes for every theologian when he must depend completely upon the Scripture and no longer upon his teachers, when he becomes answerable before the Scripture.

No one should stop with the conclusions of his teachers. It is a different matter with the Catholic priest. The evangelical pastor is answerable to the Scripture. He must be able to establish scriptural evidence for his thinking. To do so he must be mature. The sectarians embarrass us when we enter into controversy with them over the misuse of scriptural evidence. On the average they know the Scriptures better than we do. We need a better knowledge of the individual parts of the Scripture as well as of the whole. The study of the Scripture should be a part of our daily work even in the midst of the most pressing engagements. To do so will likely save us time in the long run.

5. The Scripture in prayer. The prayer-desk has disappeared from our offices. Luther, however, had one. The exegetical preacher must be grounded in the Scriptures. He must take time for prayerful consideration of the Scripture. The word itself should speak to him without its purpose being misunderstood. (Acts 6:2–4, *proseuche* and *diakonia tou logou!*) The pastor must pray more than the congregation. He has more to pray for. He needs the strengthening of his faith and the illumination of

his understanding. Prayerful consideration of the Scripture gives him a firm footing. It makes him certain of what he should pray for. He needs this prayerful refuge when he does not see how he can go on anymore and Satan tries to tear his faith out of his heart. He needs it before every hour of decision-making. He needs the study of the Scriptures when he feels inadequate and unable to pray. It drives him to the cross which Christ bore and brings that which bothers him and from which he suffers into proper perspective.

Every day should begin with meditation on the Scriptures. Before we meet men, we should meet Christ. Before we decide something, his decision should have confronted us. This kind of scriptural study is really work, not something we can doze over. It is not a matter of thinking new and great thoughts, but rather of hearing the simple old thoughts and of storing their inspiration in our hearts. We are neither obliged nor entitled to have something unusual happen in our prayerful reading of the Bible. We do not await special happenings or experiences. We only have the commission to do this work. God intends that his Word should be read and prayed over. We leave it up to him what he will make out of it. In this work the pastor must only be faithful and obedient.

[1935–1937, 1938/39]

7

How Does a Sermon Begin?

This section deals with various helps, suggestions, and correctives.

1. The work on the sermon begins with prayer over the opened text. For the sermon is not a discourse in which I develop my thoughts; it is not my word but God's own word. So I ask the Holy Spirit that he might speak. "Come, God, and receive men through thy word which you have allowed to come

from my mouth." This prayer is not merely a devotional matter, it is a part of the essential arrangement of sermon work.

2. This prayer leads to the meditation, "Accept Thou this word." Often our most familiar section of Scripture is not really God's word for the congregation. This meditation is not a mere gathering of our thoughts, it involves the assimilation of the text word-for-word. This occurs without our having established any specific objective for it beforehand. (In the Roman church, unspecified meditation was called the Solipsian meditation, which contrasted with the specified, or Ignatian meditation, which meditated upon a specific object.) It is a matter of retaining these words, as Mary did as she "pondered them in her heart" (Luke 2:19). These words should be read as if they were completely new, sent personally to us. They do not approach us at an objective distance, but rather as words which come to us from the person of Jesus and are therefore burning issues for us (Kierkegaard: "Read them like a love letter"). After the right kind of meditation, the words we have meditated upon come to us ever and again of themselves; they come to us without any conscious mental effort on our part.

3. The text should be analyzed by asking specific questions: (a) What does it tell us concerning God? (b) What concerning man? (c) What does it say to me? (d) What concerning me? (e) Where am I in danger of being untrue to the wider significance of the text? Is it because it is too hard for me; or because I want to *say* what it says but not *do* what it says; or because I do not want to believe it personally (Deut. 4:2). Any compromise of the text at this point, anything unworthy, is a great evil. How the Sermon on the Mount is mishandled in evangelical pulpits through compromise! (f) What does the text say about the church of Christ in general? (g) What does it say about my congregation in particular? (h) What to the individual whose needs and temptations I am carrying about with me from my pastoral ministry? (i) In which situations may I recognize Satan, against whom this text is directed in particular?

4. With this kind of repeated questioning and rereading, the text begins to take shape. We begin to "see" it, and it arranges

itself in manifold thoughts and pictures. When we have "seen," then we can speak freely. The effort required to achieve this result must be expended without question. But it rewards us with joy when we begin to see. Then the center of the text becomes visible. Every text has a center whether I present the text thematically or as a homily. Even a homily is not possible without this central point. This central concept may or may not be formulated into a subject. If it is so formulated, it is not absolutely necessary to refer to it. But it must be recognized. In the practical construction of the sermon it may be stated as the central thought, but the entire sermon can also direct itself toward this focal point without ever mentioning it.

In any case, it is essential that the sermon be along one sector of a circle about this middle point. On another occasion, another sermon may deal with still another sector along the circle about the same middle point. Out from this center, then, the text breaks down into a structure in which all of the individual parts are arranged and find their place.

5. Practical suggestions:

(a) It is a good idea to write the sermon during the daylight hours. Anything written at night often cannot stand the bright light of day and looks strange in the morning.

(b) The sermon should not be written all at once, but rather build a few pauses into your work. If not, the preacher runs the danger of running ahead of himself.

(c) Once the preacher has selected a text, he should stick with it and not change it after a couple of hours.

(d) The preacher should not read other sermons on his text before his own outline is completed. If he does, he becomes dependent on the thoughts of others, which makes the way to mature proclamation difficult. The reading of other sermons leads to vanity. When this occurs, preaching becomes a performance. Nothing is more dangerous to preaching than this.

(e) No sermon should be produced without use of the original text. The preacher should make an exegesis, using his lexicon and concordance, prior to the use of commentaries. For historical matters the Lietzmann Commentary is to be recommended. For theological questions, refer to Luther (his sermons may nevertheless be read beforehand now and then with advantage!) and Calvin, Bengel's *Gnomon,* Kohlbrügge and Vilmar, Schlatter. Commentary work probably belongs between the above-mentioned points three and four; i.e., between one's own analytical questions and the establishment of the central point of the text and the outline.

(f) The writing of the sermon should only begin after the preacher has placed his thoughts in a clear outline. That is a help for learning. A sermon that is difficult to learn is not a good one; at least, it is not a clear one.

(g) It is a good rule to begin the sermon at the latest on Tuesday and to conclude it at the latest on Friday. The preacher should seek his text on Sunday and have it decided upon by Monday. The usual sermon prepared on Saturday evening reveals an attitude that is unworthy of the work. Twelve hours' work on a sermon is a good general rule.

(h) The Christmas sermon should be started no earlier than four weeks before Christmas so that it will not be a message that is not in the Christmas spirit, which would be hard to explain. The same thing is true of Easter and Pentecost sermons. By the first Sunday of Advent, the texts for all four of the Sundays of Advent must be pinned down.

(i) The memorization of the sermon is not the learning by heart of exact words, but of thoughts. The preacher may memorize thought-groups. Then the words take care of themselves. The first and the last sentences of a section may be noted in a particular way. Taking a sheet of brief notes into the pulpit also has doubtful value.

(j) The day before the sermon should be kept free, at least the afternoon and evening. The pastor should best let the congregation know in advance that he does not go out on Saturday evenings and that he is not available.

(k) Once a sermon is written and thus committed to memory it is still not a sermon. Bezzel says that the sermon must be twice-born, once in the study and once in the pulpit. Everything that happens in the study is only preparation for the genuine birth of the sermon in the pulpit. The congregation does not want to be shown a child which was born in the study. The work of sermon preparation should set free the hour in the pulpit and not hinder it or lead to fear. The quality of his preparation will determine how much concentration the preacher can develop in the pulpit. Good preparation allows the greatest amount of factual, direct preaching from the pulpit. Only the unprepared preacher has to use the techniques of emotionalism, shouting, or exercising influence through pressure. These techniques betray his insecurity.

(1) Before the sermon should come Luther's sacristy prayer; kneeling-down has its place in the vestry. In the pulpit it is a questionable matter. The sermon should close with a quiet prayer that the Holy Spirit will honor this word by his presence and bring forth fruit from it. The preacher should not avoid using the vestry in preferring rather to sit among the congregation. The preacher has his particular task and must bear willingly some differences from the congregation.

Supplement:

If the sermon is prepared too soon, it perishes like the manna in the wilderness.

The preacher has to learn by strict time management to do many things at the same time and to keep one from infringing on the other.

The preacher should not avoid writing out his sermon. Adolf von Harnack said, "My pen is much wiser than my head."

The preacher should not allow himself to be kept from regularly studying a large theological work, even if he only completes 4–5 pages a day. Theological study, such as in Kittel's Lexicon, adds to the quality of sermon preparation.

A text may also have more than one central point. The context of the text [*Perikopentext*] does not have to be completely interpreted exegetically in the sermon. Doing so often causes extraneous material to be added to the sermon. The sermon which has a clear center does not have a lot of fat in it.

The Pastor and the Worship Service

The pastor's preparation for worship begins with the selection of the text. During his prayer time he remembers daily the coming worship service as he prays for his sermon and for his hearers. Without inappropriate anxiety he also prays that more might assemble themselves for worship.

The songs and various pieces of the liturgy should not be assembled on the last day. Songs which are selected before the conclusion of the sermon-making process (not out of a song-concordance, however!) can be a great help in sermon writing. Songs sometimes allow things to be seen more clearly and said more simply. Early selection of the songs allows the singing to become an intrinsic part of the instruction of the worship service. The congregation will be aware throughout the service whether the songs and liturgy have been well prepared.

The hour of worship should be kept free from the rush and uneasiness which delayed preparation can cause. Sunday ought to be a day of joy for the pastor and not one of fatigue and heated exertion. The morning of the worship service should allow time for one's own quiet reflections.

As the congregation gathers, the pastor should no longer think about his previous preparation but rather should be in prayer with the congregation either in the vestry or somewhere. He reflects upon what the week has brought to the congregation and to its various members. He gives thanks that once again he may proclaim the Gospel.

In the Course of the Worship Service:

The worship service begins with the organ prelude. When the pastor begins his ministry with a congregation he should immediately talk with the organist and come to a common understanding. The place of the organ in worship is not for the honor of the organist and the glory of music, but rather to accompany the singing and to direct the hearing of the congregation towards the preached word. The pastor should seek to influence the organist to play simple choral preludes and to leave off interludes between the verses, flourishes, and free improvisation. Background music should not be played during the Lord's Prayer and the benedicition. The organist should be encouraged to conduct practice sessions and church music evenings for the congregation. The pastor ought to advise him in the available literature and create a desire in him to read a church music magazine.

During the prelude and pastor should take his place in the vestry or in the congregation. Too much going back and forth is reminiscent of the entries of an actor.

The opening hymn allows wide room for choice. The selection of this hymn should take the whole service into consideration. It should have a broader application than the concluding hymn [*Predigthymn*]. Just like the so-called "main hymn," it should not anticipate the sermon too closely. Only the concluding hymn after the sermon can bring the theme of the sermon to a peak or summarize it, and it may also appropriately be somewhat longer. Songs that are too long are a particular evil with congregations whose singing is lifeless. The song board [where the song numbers are posted] cannot be long enough for some congregations.

The pastor should not move toward the altar too quickly, but naturally. It should be understood that the congregation is not to be distracted by this movement and that enough time ought to be allowed for silent prayer before the various parts of the liturgy. The liturgy must not be "marched off." The substance of this silent prayer results from a knowledge of the presence of God. For the turning to and from the altar table, the *cor ad altarem* is valid: right around it toward the congregation, left returning. The replacing of a book on the altar should not be done with a half shoulder-turn, but with a full turn.

The liturgy should not be conducted without a specific book of ritual. Otherwise the pastor becomes conceited and the congregation becomes confused. It should also be made clear that what takes place next is a matter of the words of the Scripture and the church. The congregation should be looked at calmly during the liturgy; the preacher should neither stare at the ceiling or at the floor. But he should also not have a fixed stare at the congregation as if he is counting heads and checking over who is there. He should not gaze about over the congregation, either.

The opening sentence, with the prescribed "In the name of the Father, . . ." authorizes the whole worship service. A proper opening sentence points toward the "Come, let us pray." It should not itself be a prayer-verse. It should also not be two or three different formulas put together, as Arper-Zillesen does it. Such expressions should not be glued together. The Bavarian liturgy is worth noticing. The "Introit" praises God's saving deeds. It does not arrange worship under themes such as work, peace, joy, as Arper-Zillesen attempts and thereby turns worship into an official, formal ceremony.

The congregation answers with singing. The pastor does not sing with them, but rather continues the exchange with the congregation during the entire liturgy.

If only three or four people are in worship, only a short liturgy should be conducted, consisting mainly of a prayer and the reading of the Scripture.

There follows next the confession of sins, which is not merely a general call to repentance. It is better if this confession consists of the words of the church rather than of biblical words. The words of the Scripture should be given only once, and that is during the reading of the Scripture. About three confessions of sin, which may be repeated, suffice for the worship service. The same is true for the expression of grace. The Bavarian liturgy contains good formulas for these expressions, but so does the Old Prussian liturgy. The confession closes with the request for forgiveness. The congregation does not answer with "Amen," but with "Lord, have mercy," in which the pastor should not lead out.

The expression of grace should be no absolution. The forgiveness of sins takes place through the preached word and the receiving of the sacraments.

The *salutatio* in its present arrangement cannot be understood clearly and naturally without further clarification.

The collect-prayer is based upon the Lection. It is determined *de tempore* from the Gospel. (See the excellent collection from Veit Dietrich and others.) During prayer the pastor turns toward the altar. That movement has a certain danger because of the Catholic misuse of it as a sacrificial altar. But by the right use of turning it may be shown that the one who prays for and speaks in behalf of the congregation also faces in the same direction as they do. In favor of this procedure is that turning the gaze away from the congregation allows them to relax and to concentrate. Against such a procedure is that it accentuates the cultic form. Turning toward the congregation, on the other hand, could underscore the fact that Christ stands in our midst.

There should be two readings of the Scripture, from the Old Testament and New Testament, or from the Epistles and the Gospels. These absolutely must be studied carefully beforehand. The announcement of the reading should be, "Hear the Word of God as it is written. . . ." Then follows only the announcement of the chapter, not the verse. The first reading closes with "Amen," the second with "Praised be Thou, O Christ." A connecting sentence is not neecessary, as if it were essential to tie the texts together. Really this takes away from the text. The sermon text may be contained in one of these readings.

The confession of faith should, if possible, be read in unison. The announcement, "Let us . . . with the words of the Fathers . . ." is too liberal for us today. The other formula, ". . . in the oneness of faith" is now a fiction. Other churches more often use the Nicene formula. It should be used more often, even if it is unfamiliar to the congregation. Presently only the churches of the Bavarian Union use the Apostles' Creed at this point. Luther included Ambrosius' song of praise, the *Te Deum,* among the creeds. The so-called "Biblicum" is impossible and mostly an attempt to avoid the creeds of the church. The congregation closes with the spoken "Amen" when it has said the Creed together with the pastor, or with the sung "Amen," when the pastor alone has said the confession.

After the creed the pastor turns himself to the altar to lay down the Bible or the liturgy book. The content of the silent prayer during this time is the remembrance of our unity with all congregations and pastors in the worship services of the day, particularly in the event of preaching in the land.

Pulpit greetings and benedictions should follow biblical expressions and are not opportunities for personally conceived additions or deviations. The text should be announced in the imperative as "Hear God's Word," not "Listen to words from. . . ."

Whether the pulpit prayer should be spoken aloud before and after the sermon is questionable. In the Reformed Church and in the English churches it is usually so. Kneeling in the pulpit to pray has dubious value. Such preparation is presupposed. It does not need to be repeated or demonstrated. If a prayer is to be said, then let it be short and spoken freely, in the sense of "Lord open my lips, and open the hearts and ears of your congregation that they may hear your word."

The announcements from the pulpit should include those things which are of significance for the entire congregation. Much effort should be devoted to these announcements. They are the life of the congregation as the body of Christ. An elder may take this responsibility, but it must be made clear to him that these announcements are a spiritual matter.

The collection cannot be regarded highly enough. When it is looked at as important by the pastor, then the congregation will also regard it as important. Occasionally the preacher should explain how much should be given. 1 Cor. 16:2, "Upon the first day of the week let every one of you lay by in store, as God has prospered him. . . ." More, or at least as much, should be given as a person spends in a week on pleasures, etc. This is not because the church needs money but for the sake of the man himself. One must also preach that the collection should be a genuine sacrifice. Even the poorest Negro in Harlem gives his dollar to the church on Sunday. When 800 people were in the church, the collection came to at least 800 dollars.

When there are announcements to be made concerning items of ministry and in cases of death, a prayer from the pulpit should not follow at once. Rather, when circumstances clearly warrant, an appropriate insertion should be made into the list of names in the requests during the prayer for the church. When our names are presented in the larger prayer for the church, it is made clearer to the congregation that real men are being prayed for.

The congregation should remain seated for the longer pastoral prayer. A set form which could be repeated now and then is advisable for this prayer. To this prayer belongs the prayer for the ruling authorities. This is not the place to make announcements to the congregation. It may not be used as an instrument for the confession of, or the confession against, Hitler. Does one pray for "the authorities" or for "the Führer"? In this case the prayer should deal first with thanks that the government still exists and that authority is there. Second, a request should be made that the government will rule according to God's will, that it might create a quiet and peaceful life for the congregation, and that this power might come under the Word of God and not hinder God's Word. Third, there should be prayer for one's enemies.

The Lord's Prayer should be read in unison as much as possible. The Aaronic blessing will only be weakened by singing a following verse of a song in place of the proper three-fold Amen. This song should be omitted. Perhaps occasionally in place of the three-fold Amen, Luther's "Our Father" song might be sung.

The liturgical colors have been established since the 12th century (Pius IV). For the festivals of Christ, white; for times of fasting and days of confession, violet; red is the color of the church and its festivals, green for the time of the Epiphany and Trinity. The altar cloth should not multiply the number of crosses in the church by being decorated with crosses. Since the sixth century the two lights on the altar have symbolized the two Testaments.

[*1935–1937, 1938/39*] 9

The Sermon and the Text

The sermon as a speech has as its distinguishing characteristic that it is an exposition of a biblical text. Jesus' first sermon in Luke 4 is a textual sermon. The preaching of the early church grew out of the customs of the synagogue. In the ancient church there was also definitely preaching without a text. If this was preaching which was not "according to the text," it was definitely preaching which was "according to the Scripture." Why do we preach from a text? This obligation has its only basis in the canon of the church, which decided that this collection of writings [scriptures] is the Holy Scripture in which God speaks. Since the sermon is the proclamation of the Word of God, its whole promise rests upon the assumption that it remain bound to the Scripture and the text. There are also obviously possibilities to preach sermons without texts, as for example, concerning some word of Luther's; but the promise of such preaching rests again entirely upon its accordance with the Scripture.

For the sake of the promise, that God speaks in the sermon through the exposition of the biblical texts, the text governs our endeavors. Steinmeyer said, "Never ask *what* [subject] you should preach about, but always from what [which text]!" It is not enough simply to paraphrase the text; that would be a cowardly withdrawal from the commission to proclaim the gospel of that text through one's own efforts. But in real proclamation the text is the beginning, the middle, and the end. So it is not enough to begin like this in the pulpit: *"We* are focusing *our* attention upon . . ."; it is also not factual to start with: *"We* take a word of the Holy Scripture as *our* basis . . ."; it is too self-oriented if we say, *"We* place *ourselves* beneath. . . ." Rather we should say: "The text of the sermon is written, . . ." or "We hear as it stands written. . . ."

2. The goal of the individual sermon is that the text might be orally expressed and that it, rather than the structure of the ideas, might be retained by the congregation; that it might be remembered, and not the problems proposed or the illustrations told. It is not a good sign when someone says that the sermon was beautiful or moving. It is a good sign when the congregation begin to open up their Bibles and to follow the text. This is a less deceiving indication of the work of the preacher than church attendance. Church-going must stand the test of whether or not the congregation is maturing in scriptural knowledge and in a growing ability to judge various doctrines.

3. The preacher should choose texts that are heavily laden with content. The words of this hymn apply to the sermon, "A ship is coming, loaded to its capacity; bearing the Son of God, full of grace, the eternal Word of the Father." It is not bad if the sermon leaves the impression that much more remains in the text than can be said at the moment. Texts that are so general that material from other texts must be brought in for their completion are not sermon texts. The text should explain itself on the basis of itself alone. Preacher and congregation should educate themselves to study solid texts, even difficult texts, and should not fear mental effort.

4. The text gives the sermon its form. Artificial organizational schemes and sermon forms produce pulpit orators. We don't need model sermons; sermons that are according to the text are model sermons. Introductions and conclusions as separate sermon parts are particularly to be avoided. The pastor who serves a congregation for years does not need to concern

himself with nervous introductions. The first minutes in the pulpit are the most promising moments. They should not be wasted with generalizations, but rather the preacher should immediately jump into the whole subject. The first sentence should not lead toward the subject but should lay solid hold on the people with the subject itself. Every text permits a countless number of possibilities of arrangement. The text itself is the best source of suggestions for these possibilities. To announce the outline for every sermon sounds pedantic and damages the character of the sermon as a form of witness.

5. The homily is the most demanding, but also the most factual, form for the exposition of the text. The preacher should therefore educate his congregation to follow the sermon with opened Bibles. This also implies an education for the pastor. Basically there is no difference between a Bible study and a sermon. Thematic preaching carries the danger that only the proposed problem and the suggested answer will be remembered; apologetic comes to the front and the text is ignored. But always, whether thematic sermon or homily, the final result should be that the *who,* not the *what,* of the sermon should dominate; in that which is said, HE speaks to you.

6. One should be very sparing in the use of stories, illustrations, and quotations. These shift attention [from the text] and usually there is not time for that. The preacher should especially guard against worn-out illustrations and untrue stories.

7. Strict textual preaching is the true way to overcome the constant demand for more sermons. The torment of waiting for fresh ideas disappears under serious textual work. The text has more than enough thoughts. One really only needs to say what is in it. Anyone who does that will not have to complain anymore about a scarcity of ideas. When we ask ourselves, "What shall I say today to the congregation?" we are lost. But when we ask, "What does this text say to the congregation?" we find ample support and abundant confidence. The faithfulness with which we enter into the text makes this possible.

8. Which texts should be preached? The pericopes? The *lectio continua?* Or texts of our own choosing?

(a) The ancient church read the book of Acts between Easter and Pentecost and this reading became the starting point for their sermons during that time. In the sixth century the first fixed schedules of pericopes began. Later the Lutheran pericope plan was based upon the Carolingian plan, which in turn had followed the old Roman order. Luther himself sharply criticized the old pericope plans because the article concerning justification was not clearly validated in them. The miracle stories, the healing acts of Jesus, and the Pauline admonitions are primarily featured. Large parts of the Sermon on the Mount and many parables are not presented at all. With the exception of Isaiah 53 and 60, the Old Testament is ignored.

In behalf of using a pericope plan it may be said that it teaches the pastor to involve himself with texts that are not his favorites. But there are texts that a person is not ready to preach at a certain time. The pastor should indeed practice, but not on his congregation. He must work exegetically on difficult texts. Nevertheless, the sermon itself is not a personal performance by the pastor for the purpose of displaying his ability to produce something from hard texts. The sermon is first and foremost the "joyous cry of Christ" (Luther).

By pedantically following the pericope order the preacher does not allow other portions of the Bible to be proclaimed. Instead, he should read the whole book with the thought that it wants to be preached. The modern attempt to arrive at a new pericope series acknowledges that the old series was inadequate and that its order worked against freedom. The Eisenach series of 1896 arranged various private attempts and enriched the old series, but it was not a unified theological work. More recently the Berneuchen movement has suggested a series arranged by themes. The Old Testament and key concepts of the Reformation are taken into consideration in this series.

(b) The *lectio continua* involves itself with one complete book of the Bible at a time. Therefore it has continuity. Under the influence of Calvin and Zwingli it was preferred by the Reformed Church. Luther also used it and recommended it as, for example, in his sermons on the Psalms. But he saw one difficulty in that only a few gifted preachers are able to follow such a method. He had the preachers' interests in mind when he wrote his Postills. Nevertheless, a preacher should not be afraid of continuous preaching from whole books, including even Romans and the Gospel of John. The *lectio continua* holds the middle ground between the pericope series and the free choosing of one's own texts. It is in the best interest of congregational maturity. Through the reading of devotional books and books of aphroisms based on verses of Scripture, and through the arbitrary sampling of texts, the Bible has become nothing more to the congregation than a fragmented anthology of sayings. This tendency must be opposed, since the Scripture is a unity.

(c) Texts come easily to the one who reads frequently in the Bible. A great portion of the Bible is lost to the preacher who preaches exclusively from the pericope series. A preacher should always enjoy preaching more than once on a particular text. Naturally this also presents the danger that the preacher will just continually circle around his pet ideas. So this rule might be suggested: Anyone who reads very frequently and very thoroughly in the Bible may also preach from texts of his own choosing. As much as possible the preacher should avoid the practice of putting two texts together and stick with only one text.

Sermons from the Apocrypha should be the exception. One should also be warned about preaching sermons on the Lord's Prayer because of the high demands placed on sermons based on this daily prayer. The Lord's Prayer should not be used catechetically either.

There have always been sermons on various parts of the Apostles' Creed or the Augustinian Confession, but perhaps they fit better into the so-called auxiliary worship services or Bible studies. Luther preached from the Apocrypha in the afternoon.

The Old Testament must once again be preached much more often. For Luther it was a relevant part of the Holy Scripture, although he saw the New Testament as the glad tidings of the fulfillment of the Scripture. Schleiermacher, on the other hand, refused to preach from the Old Testament.

Basically every biblical text is the text for a sermon, provided it is taken in its logical context and is not a meaningless fragment by itself, and to the extent that the preacher is able to understand it as the Word of God. In every text stands the One God; in every text the same God speaks. He speaks in Romans 13 as well as in Acts 5:29.

[*1935–1939*] 10

The Form of the Sermon

A. Forms for the Communication of the Sermon Material

1. Augustine listed three characteristics of his homiletics (*de doctrina christiana*) based upon the rhetoric of Cicero: to teach, to inspire, and to motivate (IV, 12–27). The Word addresses itself to the understanding, the willing, and the obedient heart of the hearer. Each of these in turn suggests elements of a lecture, of a work of art, and of an appeal; or in modern form they suggest the doctrinal sermon, the inspirational sermon, and the evangelistic sermon. Augustine's ideas on style followed those of Cicero: the speaker should be *subtile in probando* (clear, factual); *modicum in delectando* (balanced); and *vehemens in flectendo* (forceful). With the first of these qualities the preacher gains attention for his teaching, with the last—not applause—but rather a moving to tears. In any case Augustine is not talking about merely stirring up emotions, or advocating a false spirituality, but about a strict factuality: it is truth which accomplishes these actions (*ut veritas poteat, placeat, moveat*). Every sermon contains something of the following characteris-

tics, at times more of one than of another: education; inspiration; conversion. This Augustinian system later became widely influential.

2. Andreas Gerhard Hyperius (1511–1564)—besides Melanchthon the first Protestant homiletician, whose thinking was foundational for the preaching theory of Protestantism—took up the Augustinian formulation in a modified way in *De Formandi's concionibus sacris* (1533). Sermon material should be *utilis* (practical), *facilis* (understandable), and *necessarius* (essential). This material may be divided into three categories, *gnostikon, praktikon,* and *parakletikon.* The aims of these categories were described as that of *fines docendi* (the goal of teaching), *fines delectandi* (the goal of edification), *fines movendi* (the goal of moving to action). Within *finis delectandi* Hyperius included the preaching of the Gospels at Christmas, Easter, and Pentecost, which denoted a shift from the concepts of Augustine. The influence of the rhetoric of Cicero continued to hold sway over everything, however. Basically the psychological divisions of understanding, will, and feeling dominated. The category among these which is the most interesting and genuinely evangelical is that of *parakletikon.*

3. The three elements of education, inspiration, and conversion must be present in every sermon but not as three separate parts of the presentation. They stand imperceptibly behind the sermon. At certain times and for certain purposes one may completely dominate over the others.

(a) The doctrinal sermon. It has its biblical origin in the *didache;* its confessional basis is the *pure docetur* of the Augustinian Confession. But doctrine must remain the servant of the text which is being preached. Every text has its own relationship to *didache.* In times of doctrinal confusion an effort to counter false teachings must come to the foreground, and therefore also the doctrinal nature of the texts which we preach will be prominent. Nevertheless, the doctrinal sermon must not be played off against the textual sermon. Organically, the doctrinal sermon actually belongs in the catechetical instruction for adults or to the other extra events which particularly serve to develop the maturity of the congregation. Doctrine is a part of the gospel, but the gospel is not doctrine. The gospel is the revelation and act of God. The sermon should guard itself against dogmatic development. The textual sermon provides the basis for the doctrinal element in preaching, the text determines how much doctrine should appear in any one sermon. The sermons of Kohlbrügge are largely examples of doctrinal sermons, but other examples can be found in the work of Fendt.

(b) The inspirational sermon. The category *delectandi* has its justification in the right of the hearer to participate in all of the joy which the service of the gospel provides. The role of this category is that of developing the true piety and spiritual healthiness of the worship service. The purely inspirational sermon magnified delight rather than truth and exaltation rather than decision. Nevertheless, it would be overly severe if we became basically suspicious of that which brings joy.

(c) The evangelistic sermon. The evangelistic sermon has its specific theological basis in the call to repentance of the Gospels. It is particularly important for this kind of sermon to use textual preaching. In evangelistic preaching there always lurks the dangerous mistake of preaching as if I am the one who calls to repentance, while in fact only God through his Word can call anyone to repentance. The text must dominate and not my decision that "now it's time to call the people to repentance and conversion." When *I* convert, then I convert to my own way of thinking. Only God converts to God. Perhaps we can effect certain changes in people, but no more. We have a mental image of how a converted person ought to look. So we make him according to our image and ruin everything God intended. It can even be a kind of "Christianity" to which we convert him; but there is also a "Christian" godlessness. Urgent insistence exercises psychological pressure and betrays the Spirit (*pneuma*).

Conversion can have results just like political propaganda. There have been conversions to Hitler that are exactly analogous to some "conversions" to Christ. This phenomenon can occur in the preaching of Christian evangelists. In the case of such conversions a falling away inevitably follows. The person "converted" was swept off of his feet and later all he feels is embarrassment. Then it is doubly difficult to bring him back to a healthy religious position. An apparent conversion is a dangerous menace for Christians. It is not simple to distinguish between "psyche" and "pneuma." Generally speaking, both have their place. But where we see raw psychology at work, we must oppose it.

The young preacher who thinks that he must produce conversions is mistaken. He should leave the converting to God. The urging, demanding evangelistic sermon is caused by a zeal based upon a false, preconceived understanding of man. This danger can be prevented when the text is understood and preached as God's own Word. The sinister thing is that one can use his Word in a demonically suggestive way without knowing it. Dangerous, destructive powers surround the pulpit orator. Anyone who consciously works with his psychological capabilities can, with the help of the devil, become a great "evangelistic" preacher. If the preacher wants to be certain about the truth of his preaching he should devote himself exclusively to the word of the text.

There is a reason for division of labor in the church according to the various gifts. There were various ministries in the New Testament church. That was not for the purpose of dividing the work but because of the different gifts (*charismata*) which God gave his congregation. Each one had only one charisma. The ever-increasing accumulation of responsibilities and ministries of the contemporary ministry has not resulted in the strengthening but the limiting of proclamation. The Inner Mission movement (*Innere Mission*) has created the concept among us that there should be particular persons as evangelists. This concept has occasionally been strongly church-oriented among such men as Schrenk, Stöcker, and S. Keller, among others; and it has also expressed itself as a strongly sectarian movement among such men as P. Modersohn, Viebahn, and many others. The latter were largely influenced by the Anglo-Saxon "Awakening" movements.

The evangelistic sermon is concerned with conversion. According to the New Testament, proclamation results in peace through Christ (Acts 10:36), the forgiveness of sins (Acts 13:38), the way of salvation (Acts 16:17). Furthermore, it does not happen because of lofty words of wisdom (1 Cor. 2:1), it can be a profession by which a man may support himself (1 Cor. 9:14), it is a message that proclaims the death of Christ (1 Cor. 11:26), it may come from pure or impure motives, if only Christ be proclaimed, (Phil. 1:18), it testifies to what we have seen and heard (1 John 1:3, 5). In the New Testament proclamation is often presented as an uncontainable, objective event: Jesus charged them not to tell others, but the more he forbade it, the more it spread.

Excursus: Concerning the National Mission Movement

How shall our present National Mission Movement [*Volksmission*] be evaluated? What is its task; what are its limits?[1]

1. The gospel should be preached to all the world, and the Word of God should be sent forth daily. Wherever the preaching of Christ is rejected the preacher should shake the dust of that town from his feet.

2. The promise is indeed valid that God's Word continually creates a congregation for itself, but not that it will specifically convert the German people. Our responsibility to the nation consists in the proclamation of the Word and the warning of the godless. Beyond that we cannot say anything, and we cannot force anything to happen, either. We must leave everything up to the Word.

3. The preaching of the National Mission effort must under all circumstances be the whole Word, the Word of the crucified and risen Lord. There must be no fragmentation here. The whole Word alone is its source of power.

4. The National Mission movement today in Germany is a questionable undertaking. On the one hand, this tormenting question cannot be pushed aside—have the people already

1. W.S. 1936–37.

heard the message and rejected it? Is it indeed the wrath of God that has created such hardness of heart? If we are to conduct a National Mission effort, then we can only do it with this troubling question before us. On the other hand, we can no longer preach as we preached to the heathen. If we did so, it would be a despising of the goodness of God who to this hour in every city and village allows the proclamation of the gospel to issue forth. It would thus be a denial of the preaching of the church as if its preaching is no longer gospel, even though at times that is often true. That would mean, however, a dangerous over-estimation of our own words. We have never been given a promise, nor is it valid, to say "Neukölln for Christ" [a section of Berlin], or even more, "the German nation for Christ."

5. This National Mission effort is being conducted by us largely because our present church worship services are generally lacking in missionary power. That is partly the fault of the liturgy, which demands a thorough and knowledgable faith. It is partly the fault of nonmissionary sermons. Many people in the churches actually know nothing of Christ. The National Mission effort is a ministry to them in that we preach Christ to them as a matter for decision.

6. For this kind of proclamation there should be more than one preacher; there should be several, a brotherhood of them. Most of the time we do not pay any attention to the fact that the disciples were sent out by twos. Paul also always traveled with one or more others. How hard it was for him to be alone! There is promise in bearing the burden of temptation in proclamation with brothers who are united in prayer, confession, and forgiveness. This partnership is necessary in order to call the nucleus of a particular congregation to their responsibility to be examples, because these are the people who in turn must take over the follow-up work. The pastor cannot do this alone.

7. The peculiar special effort of a National Mission is a dangerous undertaking. It must recognize that a judgment is made on the basis of the word which is put out; it reminds us of

Luther's expression concerning the spot rain which comes quickly but also goes quickly.

8. The Oxford Group Movement has taken notice of the modern discontent with the theoretical aspects of the sermon and has emphasized a new vitality in the public personal testimony of the experience of salvation. The danger, however, is obvious that this vitality itself may be confused with the One who is Life. I am not expected primarily to testify emphatically to my salvation but to the Savior. I cannot save anybody with my human experience. The Savior saves. A fellowship of common witness concerning the Savior helps to correct the psychological emphasis through a spiritual one (*pneumatische*). Excessive enthusiasm on the part of any of the witnesses quickly becomes obvious. The demand for this vivacious cheerfulness is at best ambiguous. It may well be that behind a serious face there lies a happy spirit. The true joyfulness of salvation is always surrounded by temptation. This temptation teaches us to give heed to the Word.

9. The concern of the group movement is of a pastoral sort, and it can only be considered as such. The group says quite pointedly, however, that the church is its primary concern. But what they mean by "church" makes us think when we see their total confessional indifference. Their basic points are "surrender," "recompensation," and "sharing" in the things of faith. The one who has surrendered himself holds a daily "quiet time" under "guidance." Thus life is altered inwardly through the four "Absolutes," love, truth, unselfishness, and purity. These four absolutes are not intended to show us our sins but rather are regarded as attainable possibilities.

What takes place in the group movement reflects to a large measure the spirit of the times: the *élan vital,* the joy of living, the immediacy of God, the dynamic of the religious. The picture of the isolated, tempted Christian who can see nothing in himself but sin and need, disappears. Related to this problem is the fact that the preaching of the Crucified One is only weakly emphasized by the group, and that scriptural preaching is replaced by personal testimony of conversion. But it is exactly at this point that our watchfulness and our work must begin if we are to begin proclamation among groups for the National Mission effort. Or else, what has begun in Spirit will end in flesh. It is no accident that today so many "troubled people" from the German Christians and other suspected groups meet together with the group movement in England. The Lord's Supper provides for them "vitality for life," according to the Oxford Movement. But we need the Holy Spirit, not vitality for life.

B. Language in Worship

1. Because the spoken word in the Lutheran Church does not present a mystery or a holy drama as in the Roman Church —that is, it does not represent something else, but rather is the thing itself—therefore it has a particular significance for the Lutheran Church. In the Roman worship every action is exactly specified as to its performance in order to preserve the significance intended; a mistake is a transgression against the presence of God. In Protestant worship our speaking is subject to the commandments of the Word. In its spoken form the Word is the specific central point of our church. Therefore our speaking is open to danger and must be disciplined. Because the Word is able to triumph, reign, and comfort, it is necessary for us to recognize that rules of language, learn what they are, and follow them.

2. These laws may be at least set forth negatively. To be sure, the subject is a delicate one and open to misunderstanding. Until now, really helpful work concerning these principles has been lacking. Our thinking and practice has swung back and forth between the relative objectivity or subjectivity of language in worship. The problem is that in Protestant thought the objectivity of the Word of God only exists in the subjectivity of speaking men. Thereby at times objectivity and subjectivity become opposites; the objectivity of the Word of God over against the preacher and the congregation, and the objectivity of the congregation over against the individual preacher; or the

subjectivity of the preacher as over against the Word, and the objectivity of the collective congregation as opposed to subjectivity. With the knowledge that he stands as an individual before the congregation and as a man before God, the preacher must ask himself, how as a man do I speak the Word of God and how do I speak as an individual before and for the collective congregation?

3. False subjectivity, or language determined by one's personal viewpoint.

It is often possible by the first word of the liturgy to tell what sort of theology the pastor has. His theology shapes his language and his manner of speaking. An idealistic-moralistic theology results in a loud and declamatory delivery. The representatives of this method avoid the simple forms of prayer. For example, "In the name of the Father . . ." and the pulpit greetings can never be carried out simply. The prayer of adoration may be able to stand such amplification but the simpler prayers cannot.

A revivalistic-pietistic theology stumbles over the creed and the Scripture reading. It cannot abide their "churchlyness" and objectivity. With sepulchral tones, (which may already appear by the time of the Confession of Sins), a false dramatization is produced. An apologetically-oriented theology which must apologize for its own existence alternates its note of rhetorical persuasion with various devices which are intended to make the liturgy more appealing. This approach is the victim of the false notion that by the use of artistic speech techniques we can add a little something extra to preaching.

A cultic theology parades its ceremonial language. In every case the spoken word is made to serve a particular purpose which is foreign to its own intrinsic meaning. The speaker uses the spoken word as his tool. The subject interprets, shapes, and forms his object through the medium of language. The religiousity or the piousness of the preacher interprets the faith of the church. His speech interprets the Word and no longer has confidence in the spontaneous movement and power of the Word.

4. False objectivity, or cultic language.

Sometimes the subjective element in speech is consciously

and strenuously avoided. This is false objectivity, and it can go so far as to long after its classical ideal, the Latin language of the Roman mass. For the Holy Place the spoken word is no longer regarded as appropriate, a chanted tone is required. Through the use of this musical vehicle the Word moves closer to objectification. This attempt is anchored in a particular understanding of dogmatics—behind this excluding of subjectivity stands the concept of *ex opere operato* (that which works without being worked). Everything is imagined to happen objectively, without a subject being involved at all. But the Word intends that it should be spoken by a man and not an institution. True objectification is not achieved in this way at all but is really missed entirely.

5. True subjectivity, or humility.

As a Protestant preacher I am in fact the one who speaks the Word of God. As this speaker I am what I am, and I must not attempt to be anything else.

(a) The relationship of the speaker to the Word of God.

False subjectivity consists in not having confidence in the Word. The speaking which the preacher does during the worship service is different from all other speaking, in that apart from the aims of the speaker God has his own purposes in his Word which only he can provide. The Word does not need to be made alive. Our speaking must become clearly independent of our own personal aims because God must speak through it. This inherent life of the Word itself must be audible every time the Word is spoken. In the proper sense, God is the one who speaks, not us. We must make room in every speech for the inherent purpose of the Word itself. The fact that we are not identical with the actual One who brings the Word should be expressed both in the liturgy and in the sermon.

Again, we may take as an example our being deeply involved in the reading of a letter which another has written. In secular speeches—for example, political speeches—everything hangs upon the discernible *identity* between the speaker and his words. In the delivery of the divine Word, however, everything depends upon the discernible *distance*. When we read or preach words of wrath from the prophets, it must be obvious that it is not we who are angry, but God. To be sure, it is not God himself who stands before the altar or behind the pulpit and expresses his wrath, we remain the ones who stand there—but it must be plain that we ourselves stand under this wrath. The same is true in the case of the admonitions in the Epistles. We do not enter into the emotions of the letter writer which we find in the Epistles and begin to act out his part, but we ourselves listen and fear even as we read it. In secular speeches men conceal their faults by their words and hide themselves behind their grand programs of action. By doing so they hope to speak as persuasively as possible. Apparently either we cannot or we do not want to speak the truth. We are never entirely ourselves when we speak—even though we may really try to be authentically ourselves, we are at best ambiguous. In the speaking of the Word of God in the liturgy and the sermon it must be made clear that through this same Word we are revealed in all of our wickedness, and in it we become truly ourselves. That is the true, the genuinely subjective side of speaking in worship. Under no circumstances may this subjective element be obscured; that is, that we as the ones who speak also stand beneath the truth and are both judged and sustained by it. Thus our speaking must take place in complete truthfulness and factuality, with the humility which is appropriate to the Word of God.

Our humility with reference to the separation between ourselves and the Word is no virtue of ours, it is not a matter of a humble-sounding inflection, and it does not produce a particular type of preacher-personality. It is the only appropriate subjective attitude with reference to the Word. Everything depends upon this subjectivity; one's whole comprehension of the sermon is influenced by it. Preaching is not a matter of an artistic presentation; but rather it is occupied with man in his sin and need, confronted and encouraged by the Word. Actually we become involved in a higher and more genuine form of participation in the Word when we allow our own subjectivity to die.

(b) The relationship of the speaker to the congregation.

The pastor errs when he thinks that he represents individuality in contrast to the collectivity of the congregation; or accordingly, as if the liturgy had to present the collective side of worship and the sermon the individual side. We are not dealing with a performance, but with service. No part of the worship service is the exclusive expression of an individual. In the various prayers it is not essential to allow the congregation to participate in order to prevent exclusiveness. The only true distinction between the individual who does the talking in the service and the collectivity of the congregation is a matter of distinctive service. The individual who stands before the congregation only has the right to serve the congregation, and the spotlight must never be upon the individual as such. He is not entitled to his own peculiar emphases and demands.

But of course the pastor should, and can, serve the congregation as the person he really is, with his own individuality. Here the concept of genuineness becomes important, a genuineness which is committed to service and is disciplined (Col. 2:23). Everything unnatural and artificial hinders the preacher's credibility and stands as a lie in the way of the Word. It is unnatural to prevent naturalness. Genuineness is the opposite of pretentiousness and of the attitude of "letting one's self go." In the service of Jesus I become natural. I stand at the altar and at the pulpit as the person that I really am, and I imitate no one and nothing. The Word is indeed contrary to our nature, but it does not make us unnatural. Where unnaturalness exists, there also exists a false relationship to the Word. If humility is the proper attitude for the speaker with reference to God and his Word, then genuineness, in its truest sense, is the proper attitude of the speaker with reference to the congregation.

6. From what has been said about factuality, humility, and discipline, it would be a false conclusion to elevate monotony and rigidity to the ideal. It is true that certain psychological approaches result from these theological categories. Truthfulness and factuality suggest simple methods. They discourage senseless shouting and emotional excitement in preaching and

worship. We are witnesses, not the trumpeters of the Last Judgment. That does not, however, exclude from our witness the utmost zeal but rather includes it. We are not talking about a phlegmatic, but a passionate, factuality. Indeed, in the discipline of factuality, personal excitement may also occur. The matter has a right to demand our passion. There is even the right for a certain amount of pathos in our speaking as well. Of course not a pathos which flogs the thing to death, but the kind which has a zeal for the subject. The Word of God demands a great deal of reserve and awe, but it demands an even greater confidence and joyfulness in its power and might.

7. And now a particular word concerning preparation for worship. The preparation of the Word is as much demanded as the preparation of gestures and rhetorical tricks is forbidden. Gestures are pictures. The sermon, however, is the presence in words of the God who is not portrayable. Gestures and rhetoric may accompany the sermon in an unpremeditated way as a genuine expression of subjectivity, but they may not be depended upon to carry the sermon. The preacher cannot learn to speak from politicians or actors. Each kind of speech demands its own characteristic passion; it cannot be transferred from one subject to another. The sermon is to be prepared to the point of organization but not to the point of declamation. To do so would result in the loss of truthfulness and genuineness. This sets the limits for the degree of one's preparation. The sermon must be born at the pulpit. The person who may be a bad speaker, measured by other standards, but preaches according to the gift given him, can and will have great spiritual effectiveness.

8. Should the preacher develop preaching style?

A preacher should not set this as his goal. It leads to vanity and after a while it makes preaching boring. "Style" in this sense is inappropriate to the matter at hand. It is self-directed and seeks to be recognized and approved for itself. It is unfortunate when gifted preachers develop a "style." Styles are indeed unavoidable, but they should not be sought after. Perhaps it is only possible to describe negatively the necessary attention which the preacher must devote to his choice of words. The following description is given with the knowledge that being made aware of our responsibility for our own words exposes us to the danger of a destructive self-consciousness. But perhaps the following may be said:

(a) The preacher should not employ the language of the popular orator who wants to talk his listeners into something. Nor the language of the propagandist who subordinates his words to suit his particular purposes. One should avoid superlatives, appeals, and exclamations because they quickly lead to the false identification of the Word with a spectacle. God's Word does not need exclamation marks in the sermon. The Word of God itself is the exclamation mark.

(b) The preacher should be careful not to fall into the language of the lecturer who continually develops new thought-sequences and gets involved in deductions and inferences, such as "at this point the following objection might be raised." This suggests a false distance relative to the Word.

(c) The preacher should not speak the "language of Zion" of the pious person and should avoid poetic, fantastic, and extravagant imagery. The detailed coloring-in of biblical situations ("the towering cross") and human conditions (such as descriptions of sins) should be excluded. This brings a false subjectivity into play.

(d) The preacher should not use the sacramental language of the sanctuary, or that of dogmatics, either. Elevated speech results from a false objectivity. It betrays an improper relationship to the congregation.

(e) The preacher should not "let himself go" and use the language of the street. A conscious popularization of language and the use of slang reveals a false understanding of genuineness. By doing so we do not become popular, but common.

Nevertheless, to attempt to say something positive about who and what should determine language, the language of Luther's translation of the Bible should be studied. The most extreme restraint and conciseness of language is appropriate for the sermon. Every superfluous word causes the Word to become inaudible among so many words. Natural language is language that does not allow itself to be determined or embellished by anything except by that subject with which it deals. Factuality and genuineness are the positive characteristics of language in worship which might be mentioned here.

[*1935–1937, 1938/39*] **11**

After the Sermon

1. If the sermon is not to be understood as a performance which concludes with the last spoken word, then it is apparent that the time after the sermon is as much a part of it as the time before it. The sermon from the pulpit concludes with a prayer which is spoken aloud (or, better, spoken softly!). It should consist of three elements: first, humble gratitude that God has honored the preacher by allowing him to proclaim the Gospel and to be the shepherd of the congregation; next, a request for the forgiveness of those sins which have occurred through vanity and laziness, through misunderstanding and inattentiveness to the divine Word; and finally, a request that God might now allow his Word to have free movement throughout the congregation to do its promised work.

2. There is no greater liberation from the restlessness which comes to the preacher following his preaching than when the pastor follows his sermon by serving the Lord's Supper. In the serving of the Supper he is truly the instrument of the God whose Word he had to preach. He is set free from fears concerning his own subjectivity and is completely one with the church and upheld by it. He accepts the grace that he may re-

main a servant of this Word in spite of his sins. It is a real shame that this Supper continues to be the exception in the services of our churches. Our anxiety after the sermon would otherwise be very easy to allay.

3. After the sermon, the pastor needs pastoral care. At that time he stands in danger of several things. Affected by an uneasiness which seems inherent to the period following the sermon, he is impelled to seek a conversation which will minister to him. Since usually there is not a formal opportunity provided for that within the congregation, he tried to get rid of this restlessness in meaningless conversations with friends, or else he nervously questions others as to their opinion of how things went. A favorable judgment will satisfy his vanity. But his actual uneasiness remains unsatisfied and is only covered over.

The pastor, however, has the right to hear others discuss whether God's Word was given a place in his sermon. The solution to this problem might be a conversation in the vestry with mature members of the congregation or elders who are in a position to pray with the pastor. The congregation should be educated to the possibility of a relevant criticism of the sermon by being requested to bear a part of the responsibility for the proclamation of the Word of God. This teaches the congregation to protect the preacher from unchristian criticism and unchristian fanaticism. It will also learn to differentiate between that which the pastor really intended as comfort in his sermon and that which was misunderstood to be comfort. Petty, presumptuous criticism can be prevented in this way. Luther: "In order that a . . . congregation might have both the right and the power to judge every teaching" (1523).

The preacher's lack of peace after the sermon is also rooted in his temptation toward unbelief. When Luther said that the fifth request of the Lord's Prayer does not apply to the one who has just preached, and that he should not pray for forgiveness after the completed sermon, he intended to say, "You have done your work, leave and go and get your glass of beer and let the Word of God take its free course; God will care for that." But he did not tell that to everyone; it was only valid for the tempted one. To that one he wished to say that the Word alone is effective, not his zeal and not his restlessness.

A sense of total emptiness after the sermon indicates a mistake in preaching. The preacher should not exhaust himself. The preacher is simply a handservant, someone who helps out. The preacher does not draw from his own resources but from God's fountain. And if it should ever happen that the pastor ever does exhaust himself, this mistake should not be made worse by acting as if it were he himself who made such a great sacrifice; it is God who spends his all. God expends himself, we do not. Our physical condition may well be indicative of our spiritual condition. This complete brokenness after preaching is a sign that something spiritual is not right, and that we have been possessed by a fanaticism which caused us to preach ourselves out. The right sort of sermon should not physically exhaust us.

The worse danger, of course, is the pastor who is satisfied with himself and his sermon. He takes comfort in Luther's words of assurance and becomes a prayerless routine-follower. When that happens, no effort should be spared to drive this kind of preacher into true humility.

4. After the worship service the preacher should look at his text one more time and think it over. It is not something that should be forgotten and laid aside. During this reflection it is possible for the whole sermon to be called into question. This attitude can be resisted if the sermon is not looked upon as a performance. The text continues to be the key factor; it speaks ever and again to the preacher as the Word of God.

5. In the evening the pastor should prayerfully remember his brethren in ministry and service. The preached message will provide an important basis for the work among the congregation during the following week, in conversations and in pastoral care. Just as the sermon grows heavily out of the pastor's work among the congregation, it also provides opportunity for work among the congregation to be developed out of it.

Postscript

A. Criteria for Evaluating the Sermon

1. Faithfulness to the Scripture.

A non-textual sermon can still be faithful to the Scripture by being based upon the central message of the Bible as a whole. Luther very often preached without a text at all, but nevertheless scripturally.

2. Faithfulness to the text.

How does the sermon relate to the pastor's exegetical research? Do the individual parts of the text stand in proper relationship to each other? Has anything important been overlooked? Is the central meaning of the text apparent?

3. Faithfulness to the Confession.

Was it preached with an interpretation that is in accord with the teachings of the church, or not? That is, was the Scripture read according to the *sola fide?* Was the sermon in order doctrinally?

4. Faithfulness to the congregation.

This is the distinctive homiletical test. Questions should be asked concerning:

(a) Simplicity in speech and presentation. Has the imagery of the text been fully utilized; has too much been said in one sentence, too much sentence-packing and too many dependent clauses; or are too many literary and rhetorical intrusions employed?

(b) Transparency in construction. Even a homily needs the support of paragraphs—it is no mosaic. Did the interpretation of the text stay on the main track—going off on tangents may be appropriate for exegetical research, but not for the sermon; how well does it lend itself to being remembered and repeated?

(c) Is the direction (it might even be called the attack) of the sermon obvious, i.e., what it seeks to accomplish; where has the fight with the devil been enjoined; did everything get bogged down in a mere textual paraphrase?

5. Faithfulness to the commission (objectivity).

Has the Scripture and the church been used as an excuse to present one's own ideas? Did the religious virtuoso speak, or the one who is dedicated to the cause of Christ?

6. Genuineness (subjectivity).

This criterion is difficult to apply to the sermons of others! The preacher must ask himself, "Do I believe what I say? Or am I just making official sounds?"

7. The relationship between the new and the old.

Has the old been said in a new way? Does it cause someone to want to look again into the text? Does the sermon include the two characteristics of interpretation and witness in proper relationship to one another?

8. The relationship between the Law and the Gospel.

Has all that has been said finally degenerated into nothing more than legalism? Has the Gospel been presented so that God's liberating claim to men is audible?

B. Sources of Error

1. Do not pass judgment upon various texts such as "nice," "deep," "true," "correct," etc. We are not judges of the Scripture. We should let ourselves be judged by it!

2. Do not overemphasize the contemporary significance of the Scripture. Its present significance is presupposed. Therefore do not separate the application and explanation of the text, they belong together. Avoid saying, "This speaks exactly to you and me."

3. Do not defend the Word of God, testify to it. You are a preacher, not an apologist.

4. Do not get stuck in the summary paraphrase of the text.

At the pulpit we do not present "the theology of Apostle So-and-So"! See if you can't say "God says" where you would like to say, "the Apostle John says."

5. Guard yourself against speaking too conditionally, with too many reservations and limitations. "In Christ" there is no room for conditional sentences.

6. Do not divide the Pauline admonitions according to those which contain promise and those which contain duties [*Gabe und Aufgabe*]. Outherwise you will preach nothing but moral sermons. The Gospel is not a neuter, impersonal force to which a set of directions must be given. The gift of grace already contains within it the New Life. Within this gift there is already the presupposition of the task, and vice versa.

7. Do not use the Scripture as a club with which to beat the congregation. That is priestcraft. We are not to preach sins, but to witness to their overcoming; we are not preachers of repentance, but messengers of peace.

8. Do not indulge in the cataloging of the sins and problems within the congregation ("don't we keep on, over and over again"). Do not be deceived into interpreting our piece of history as if it were cut off from A.D. 1–30 and dealing with it separately.

9. Do not terrify men with the Last Judgment and death. Christ does not overpower, he knocks at the door. Therefore it is not appropriate for us to be so violent in the sermon.

10. Guard yourself against presenting utopian views in eschatological sermons. We preach a Mohammedan sermon when we anticipate visions of the times to come. We cannot say, "Heaven looks like this." The visions of an apocalyptic seer are not that which is promised to us in our time, but rather a view into the kingdom of faith. The eschatological word presently continues to be fulfilled in Christ alone, and in the midst of the apocalyptic pictures stands the figure of the martyred Lamb (Rev. 22).

11. Do not slave over the introduction and the conclusion of the sermon. You can commit yourself immediately to the Word. It is a ship "loaded to its capacity."